PR FOR AUTHORS

PR

FOR AUTHORS

How to use public relations, press releases, and social media to sell more books

MICHELLE CAMPBELL-SCOTT
&
NANCY HENDRICKSON

BY THE SAME AUTHORS:

Make Your Book Work Harder

How to use multiple platforms to make more money

ALSO BY MICHELLE CAMPBELL-SCOTT:

Goodreads for Authors

How to use Goodreads to promote your books

ALSO BY NANCY HENDRICKSON:

How to Write for Kindle

A non-fiction book in 72 hours or less

FREE GIFT

Visit ***http://www.forauthors.info*** to download
How to make the most of the Big 3 book cataloging sites

For Pat Flynn,
who got over 8,000 authors networking

CONTENTS

ೞ✐

INTRODUCTION

ᙣᙦ

> **90% of books fail because**
> **authors fail to promote them**
>
> Bob Mayer

MICHELLE LUCKED INTO PUBLIC RELATIONS (PR) in the bustling port city of Liverpool, England in the 1980s after being sent to a PR agency as an admin temp. She was delighted, thinking it would be a glamorous posting. Well she did have to look smart some of the time but the work couldn't really be described as glamorous.

As a PR Assistant, part of her job involved showing visiting reporters around the development site of a large International festival. A large, very muddy, rainy development site on the banks of the wind-swept River Mersey. She spent much of her first couple of weeks at the agency wearing galoshes and streaked mascara while trying to cover reporters with wind-blown umbrellas as they took notes and photographs.

The rest of the time was divided into writing press releases, addressing and mailing hundreds of envelopes, checking press cuttings, and fielding calls from clients, reporters, and editors. She loved it, even though it was hard work with long, unsociable hours.

She set about learning the ropes from a master of the game, the agency's MD. Brian Johnson has many talents but the biggest is his likeability. Michelle watched as he befriended everyone: clients, VIPs, reporters, events staff, and janitors. He treated them all the same and they warmed to him very quickly. The Queen visited the site for the opening. He was the same with her as he was with the people who cleared up after the launch party.

This was no act, though, he's a genuine people person. Imagine someone who is always delighted to see you and willing to drop everything to share a few stories over a coffee. You're imaging Brian.

That, at its most basic, is what the backbone of PR is: being available, being friendly, and being open with information in order to project your company's image.

What you really want is for other people to talk about your company/brand. You aren't advertising yourself, you are just giving the information that other people will pick up and run with.

This is bad news for many authors. If you are an author who prefers your own company to a room full of people you're not the only one. Many of us chose our craft not least because it is something we don't have to do in a group or on a committee!

Some of us also refuse to consider ourselves likeable. If you have read Susan Cain's book, *Quiet: The Power of Introverts In a World That Can't Stop Talking,* you may begin to understand what is going on here.

The first is that, if we aren't 'out there', confident, noisy extroverts, we may have been made to feel slightly inadequate by teachers and other authority figures. In her TED talk, Susan Cain tells the story of going to her first summer camp. Her mother packed her lots of books, which wasn't strange because: "In my family, reading was the primary group activity."

Susan happily went off to camp, imagining cozy evenings reading and discussing stories. She was in for a shock. She discovered that the other girls considered her too 'mellow' and camp staff were concerned about her lack of camp spirit - just because she preferred spending time with a book to being rowdy.

The camp counselor told her she should work harder at being more outgoing. She sensed that she was only acceptable to others if she was acting in an extroverted manner and that introverts were somehow wrong.

Michelle's daughter has had similar messages. She has been a voracious reader since she learned how to read at the age of 4. She always has a book with her wherever she goes and owns hundreds. She was accused of using them to escape reality.

Hmm. Isn't that what we all do, every day? When reading, writing, day-dreaming, watching TV or movies, we are escaping our own reality and stepping into someone else's ideal. Even when it comes to eating, drinking, or taking supplements (or drugs), what we are doing is attempting to 'change our state' as Tony Robbins would call it. That means changing the way we feel. Or escaping reality.

Nancy is one of those incessant personality test-takers and in almost every case she scores high on the Introvert scale. This doesn't mean she won't leave her home at Herb Cottage; it does mean that, after she's gone to a client meeting or finished doing a webinar, she craves alone time. As we know, extroverts recharge from people energy, introverts recharge from alone energy.

So we resent the implication that people who love books, who like quiet, and who are comfortable with their own company are in some way inadequate. We're not!

If you have trouble accepting/liking yourself, you may be reluctant to put yourself out there, PR-wise, going on the basis that you can't expect other people to like you if you don't like yourself. It's true, people like people like themselves. You just have to find others like yourself.

Please bear this in mind:

> *There are lots of introverts out there who like other introverts and enjoy hearing what they have to say.*

It is possible - in fact, advisable - to learn public relations and media skills, whether you are an introvert or an extrovert. You don't have to be born with them. Extroverts can sometimes seem like they are born with media skills but, actually, they often need more training than introverts. That's because they are likely to say too much, be too open, chat too candidly in front of reporters.

Being good at public relations doesn't mean you have to turn into the modern equivalent of a travelling salesman with a too-hearty laugh, a cheesy grin, and a clutch of bad jokes. It simply means three things:

- ➢ Being available.
- ➢ Putting yourself and your information out there.
- ➢ Having interesting information available about your books/ skills.

You don't need a degree/diploma in PR - you just have to 'get it'.

It is very important that you get it. Whether you are a traditionally-published author or an Indie, it is tough to sell books in the current economic climate. Many authors are complaining of reduced royalties over the last year or so.

2012 was a great year for many Indie authors, on Amazon and elsewhere. Great royalties and an open playing field as the public really took to their Kindles and the big publishing houses hadn't realized that Indie authors were getting most of the sales due to lower prices. A lot of Internet Marketers spotted that. That led to a deluge of cheap self-published books (of varying degrees of quality) flooding the market. It made it harder for authors to help potential readers find their books.

This last year has been great for some but hard slog for many. Amazon's KDP Select started to be less effective at getting books ranked, many of the sites and services promoting free and bargain books disappeared, and even the paid promotion sites became less effective and more difficult to get onto.

The solution is to keep at it, to keep writing new books and promoting existing ones. There's a lot to be gained from consistency and staying power. Authors will keep writing books long after the Internet Marketers have moved onto the next craze (it seems to be video).

The book in your hands is one of the keys you need to succeed. PR is something you can do every single day, almost without effort, to raise your profile, maintain your reputation, and get your books in front of people.

If you've ever been baffled by successful authors and book marketing experts who say that you should be promoting at least one of your books at all times, you're not alone. Many people wonder what they can do to promote their books and how much time they should spend on it.

PR is one of the most helpful things you can do and this book will show you how. The great news is that PR is [usually] free, doesn't take long, and works for you while you sleep.

Interestingly, PR not only stands for 'Public Relations', it also stands for 'PageRank'. PageRank is an algorithm which Google uses when deciding where to place websites in the rankings when people search (i.e. which page they appear on and where on the page). That's very relevant to us as authors because, by using public relations tools such as press releases (another PR word!), we will taking steps to influence the PageRank of our websites/blogs.

That's something useful we have learned from the Internet Marketers while they've been on our patch!

Let's look at what public relations is and why successful authors make sure they find out about how to use it ...

CHAPTER ONE

WHAT EXACTLY IS PUBLIC RELATIONS?

᎕᎒

WHEN YOU READ THE PHRASE 'PUBLIC relations', what pops into your mind? We asked a few people this question and the answers were varied:

- ➢ Marketing/Advertising.
- ➢ Reputation management.
- ➢ Spinning.
- ➢ Sales.
- ➢ Sending lots of press releases.
- ➢ Telephoning reporters.
- ➢ Networking.

One definition often bandied around in media circles is that PR is:

> ## "The care and feeding of reporters."

That was certainly true when Michelle worked in PR in the 1980s – she spent a lot of time buying drinks for reporters! Reporters aren't the only people we want to reach now, though. We're kind of cutting out the middle person with post-Internet PR We do still want to reach reporters but also the many, many bloggers and regular Internet users who will repost interesting content. With modern public relations we are actually aiming to reach the ***public***!

Some PR umbrella bodies spend years coming up with a definition of what PR is and it is usually along the lines of promoting a person or company's image and controlling what the media finds out about it.

There's a good definition of the website of Alexander G. Public Relations[1], a Kansas-based PR agency. It says:

> ### *Advertising buys AWARENESS; strategic public and media relations earns CREDIBILITY.*

---

[1] http://www.alexgpr.com/about/what-we-do

That's a great way of showing the differences between advertising and PR It doesn't matter how much money you throw at advertising if you don't have credibility.

After Michelle's first job in PR, she switched to advertising and was one of the account handlers of a large electricity company in the UK. They had a huge advertising budget, which they spent in national press, but they didn't spend much on PR – and it showed. It never ceased to amaze her how much money they were willing to spend on advertising but very little on customer service. Customers would constantly complain about the company's customer service and the company's answer was to chuck more money in the advertising budget! If they had diverted some of it to training their customer service staff and some to PR, they would have had happier customers, a better public image, and higher profits.

Let's look at the different aspects – real and perceived - of PR individually.

Marketing/Advertising

Marketing = the activities that are involved in making people aware of a company's products.

MERRIAM-WEBSTER DICTIONARY

Marketing is PR's conjoined twin – each unique yet intimately linked. They are both concerned with publicity.

In a company, a marketing department can incorporate the advertising and PR departments or they could be separate – it often depends on the size of the company and its need for publicity.

Publicity means telling people about your product/service, getting the news about it out there by various means. A marketing department might draw up a schedule of promotional activities and then buy in the services of an advertising agency and/or a PR agency to provide those services.

Advertising usually means paid promotional activities – such as advertisements in print publications, on radio/TV, or online ads on Google, Facebook, etc.

PR is generally concerned with more subtle publicity, often involving relationship-building and issuing press releases that provide material for reporters. Sometimes a reporter will respond to a press release with a telephone call to get more information. PR is about being available for that call, forging a mutual-trust relationship with the reporter, and having relevant information available (quickly, knowing that the reporter will be working to a deadline).

Another thing that a marketing department (or the marketing part of an author's brain!) is concerned with is coming up with offers, competitions, and events. As authors, we are used to this with KDP Select free promo days, reducing our book prices for special events, providing free copies for reviewers, book signings (physical and virtual), blog tours, and more. We know that we need to promote these activities or they fall flat.

Every author needs a good marketing plan – a schedule of activities that you intend to do in order to raise awareness of yourself as an author brand, and of your books as individual and series titles.

HOW MARKETING/ADVERTISING AFFECTS YOU:

Even if you are traditionally-published, you are in many ways responsible for your own marketing. A publisher is only going to spend a certain amount of money and a certain amount of time marketing your latest book – it probably won't do anything to push your back catalog.

Publishing houses don't have the big budgets they used to have anymore and will only lay out cash they know they are going to get a return on. That's why you will see adverts and promotions for the big celebrity authors but not the newcomers or the mid-list ones.

If you are an Indie author, the whole marketing thing is on your shoulders.

cont/d...

> There is freedom in that, of course, but some pressure too! You have to learn the ins and outs of advertising quickly or you are in danger of wasting a lot of money and sinking without trace.
>
> The bottom line is that *all* authors have to learn how to market themselves and their books. They need to promote their personal brand and build/maintain their reputation.
>
> There are a lot of books out there and a lot of authors telling people about their books. You need to market yourself and your books so that people will find them. You can do that through buying adverts (generally now that will be online, perhaps on Google or Facebook or specific sites), creating offers, alerting promotional websites about those offers, sending press releases, posting on social media, staging a virtual blog tour, or numerous other ways – all under the umbrella of marketing.

There's no point spending money on advertising if you haven't paid attention to PR, though. Yes, schedule some highly targeted ads on Facebook, take advantage of a special offer coupon from Google AdWords, do some Goodreads self-serve advertising to support a Goodreads giveaway, but don't do it without working on your PR as well, or it will be wasted money.

Reputation Management

PR guys are often portrayed as sharks on TV and in movies. In the original series of *Dallas,* J.R., the main anti-hero, hired a public relations guru/shark to rescue his oil company's image. He thought that was possible, even though he spent most of the time himself damaging the company's image. PR guys have a tarnished reputation because of this and other stereotypes, which is ironic considering what their job is all about!

People often think that PR is some sort of miracle fix when everything has gone wrong. It's true that a well-oiled PR machine can swing into action to minimize damage after a publicity stunt goes wrong, or a customer complaint is mishandled. It's much better to manage PR well before things go wrong though. Better and less expensive.

That's done through:

- ➢ Providing information for reporters, so they don't have to scrabble around elsewhere to get it and – dare we even hint it? – making some things up!
- ➢ Being very professional and protecting your own brand/image.
- ➢ Being available to answer questions so you can clarify things yourself and not allow people to guess or grasp at half-truths.

Reputation management now is often handled on social media – with varying degrees of success! Some brands and companies do a tremendous job of managing customer service via social media platforms. We'll look at several later.

HOW REPUTATION MANAGEMENT AFFECTS YOU:

As an author, this means establishing your credibility as a 'brand'. It means behaving! It means portraying yourself as you want to be seen – so no tales of drunken nights out on Facebook and no comedy photo on LinkedIn.

Some authors are tempted to jump into reputation management when they get what they consider to be a bad or unfair review on Amazon. It's tempting but something that you should never do. For starters it would make you look like an amateur – professional, successful authors don't comment on their reviews (many don't even read them). It could also risk escalating into a nasty public spat.

There's a reason why celebrities hire PR people to handle their reputations – because most people don't have the skill, tact, or experience to do it themselves.

Spinning

Max Clifford was a well-known, almost notorious, PR man. He ran a successful PR agency in the U.K. but was best known for promoting dubious news 'scoops'. (He is now better known for being convicted of a series of sexual assaults.)

He started as a reporter and took a job in the press office of EMI records. One of his first jobs was to promote The Beatles, which he obviously did quite well, as they were unheard of before he took over. Let me repeat that – The Beatles had been signed by a record label and had been playing in clubs for years but they didn't become a big hit with the public until the PR machine kicked in. Interesting.

Clifford later represented O.J. Simpson, Marvin Gaye, Frank Sinatra, Muhammad Ali, and Marlon Brando, among others.

He started on his road to notoriety when he 'spun'[2] a story about a comedian called Freddie Star. The newspaper headline read, 'Freddie Starr ate my hamster' and got widespread publicity. The comedian later admitted that the whole thing had been invented to generate publicity for his tour. That was one of the first examples of PR being used to create stories – and to gain money as stories are often sold to newspapers. That's why people sometimes associate PR with lying.

---

[2] Definition of spinning a story = to give a news story a particular emphasis or bias.
Source: http://www.oxforddictionaries.com/definition/english/spin

PR people try to dissociate themselves from that sort of behavior and say that is the work of publicists. Maybe, but the work of a publicist and the work of a PR person can look quite similar!

HOW SPINNING AFFECTS YOU:

As an author, hopefully this won't affect you because spinning stories generally backfires. The truth comes out eventually and it isn't worth the damage to your reputation to gain some temporary publicity on the back of a lie or half-truth.

Where clever PR gurus succeed, sometimes, is in giving a true news scoop to a reporter or paper in return for them running something about a client of theirs that needs publicity.

It's fairly unlikely that you will ever have access to a story that a reporter would consider newsworthy but if you do, you might be able to get them to run a piece about your book as well!

Sales

This is a misconception as PR people aren't sales people. They don't actively hit the streets or the telephones to try to get people to buy things. They are always aware of sales potential though. They will use every opportunity they can to promote their company/client – whether that is at conferences/events, to reporters, in interviews, or other means.

How Sales Affects You:

If you are traditionally published your publisher will probably have sales people to get bookstores to stock your books. They will try that for a couple of weeks – six at most. Then they will move on to push the next batch of newly-released books.

So traditionally published authors need to join the ranks of the Indies who need to keep one eye on sales opportunities at all times. Publishing house salespeople will attend conferences and get to know the book buyers; you can do the same by attending conferences and writing events.

You can approach bookstores yourself. Often a local, independent bookstore will stock an author's books simply because they are local residents.

cont/d...

> You can also network online, via social media. You won't – hopefully – be saying "Buy my book" in the way a salesperson would, but you would be putting on your PR hat and spending time making relationships, getting to know people. That's the way to make sales without being seen to be selling!

Sending Lots Of Press Releases

This is true! They used to be mailed out manually but today it is much easier thanks to the Internet. It is also easier to find suitable contacts to send press releases to.

Press releases are usually commissioned, researched, and then written – often with the help of interviews with relevant people – before being sent. They are then approved before sending out. Sending out means being sent to relevant reporters and editors. The word 'relevant' there is important. They hate getting bombarded with press releases that aren't relevant to them, yet it happens surprisingly frequently.

The U.K. has a national newspaper called the *Financial Times*. It only carries financial news, yet they get press releases about everything from the latest baby product to anti-wrinkle cream. And, no doubt, a few book launch press releases as well. That's fine if the book is a financial one, of course, but most won't be.

Blanket sending of press releases is counter-productive as it makes reporters less likely to read the ones that are relevant to them. Most of us know now how to block out things because we are all assaulted with so much information in the digital age. Reporters are the same.

HOW PRESS RELEASES AFFECT YOU:

Press releases aren't just aimed at reporters, due to much online content now being user-generated.

We put our releases 'out there' to be indexed by Google and other search engines. What we really want is to appear on page 1 of the search engine results pages (SERPs) because that is the best way to be found. Few people click past the first page of the SERPs.

A modern press release is – potentially – available forever online, rather than being a one-day wonder, as used to be the case. Now we can put our releases out via online press release distribution services that will get them indexed by search engines.
Then we can post the information everywhere online – via social media, blogs, pings, multimedia, and more.

cont/d...

We still go after reporters, though, because they remain strategically important for publicity. You will need to make lists of relevant publications/media outlets (newspapers, magazines, TV and radio stations) for each of your books and find names of reporters who work for them.

You can just send press releases to 'Newsdesk' or 'Lifestyle Editor' or whatever, but you have more chance of success at building a relationship if you can get a name.

You can send your press release to these publications/media outlets and you can also send them to online services – PR distribution services, online news directories, etc.

Try to find some reporters local to where you live as local stories often make the news more readily than they do for a national paper/station.

You should also upload your press release to your own online platforms – your website/blog and social media accounts. It's all indexed by Google and provides more social proof that you are who you say you are. It makes your books more discoverable as well.

Much more on press releases later in the book.

Telephoning Reporters

Many people think that you should follow up a press release with a telephone call. You could ... you could also visit a local zoo and punch a hungry tiger on the nose. Neither of those things is a safe idea.

Reporters are incredibly busy people and newsrooms are insane with activity, noise, and deadlines. No reporter will welcome a telephone call from every person who has sent him/her a press release – it would mean being on the telephone all day! Maybe it used to work in the past when money was less tight and newsrooms had more staff. Now, it's unthinkable.

A reporter or editor may want to talk to you after they have read your press release, if your story is of interest/relevance to them. Sometimes it takes longer than that. They may note that you are an expert at whatever and remember you in a few weeks when they're doing a relevant story. All you need to do is make sure you are available and give them lots of ways to contact you.

HOW THIS AFFECTS YOU:

It's great - just send your press releases out. Don't follow them up with telephone calls. There may be occasions when you will need to call a reporter but it won't be just to see if they got your press release.

cont/d...

> If there is a news story that is very relevant to your expertise, you may want to telephone the reporter who broke the story, to see if they would like a quote from you for a follow-up story. You could email instead, if you prefer.
>
> Do be very available so reporters can contact you. Give them every method: telephone, cellphone, business and home emails.
>
> They will sometimes try to get hold of you with just an hour's deadline for a story, wanting a quote – often at odd times of night!

Networking

Networking is just meeting people – either in the real world or online. There's a good definition of it on Entrepreneur.com[3]:

> *"The process of developing and using your contacts to increase your business, enhance your knowledge, expand your sphere of influence, or serve your community."*

---

[3] http://www.entrepreneur.com/article/225067

Wow, that really takes the pressure off as many authors get quite twitchy about the idea of networking. Sometimes they don't like it because they are a bit shy and dislike the idea of trying to sell themselves or their books.

The idea of merely expanding your contacts and sphere of influence, and enhancing your knowledge is much more appealing.

As an author, networking can help give you credibility, establish your expertise, and raise the profile of your books and yourself. It can make a massive difference to your earning potential and give you terrific contacts who you can learn from.

It can be real-world networking but it can also be virtual, online networking, in various forms.

Does the idea of networking terrify you or excite you? Many authors are quite daunted by the prospect. Don't worry if you aren't a naturally sociable/outgoing person.

Let's go back to Susan Cain again (the author of *Quiet*[4]).

After her childhood experiences of feeling that being introverted was a weakness and made her a failure, she worked hard to try to become an extrovert – or at least to convince others that she was an extrovert:

---

[4] http://amzn.com/B004J4WNL2

> *"I became a Wall Street lawyer instead of the writer that I had always longed to be – partly because I needed to prove to myself that I could be bold and assertive.*
>
> *I was always going off to crowded bars when I really would have preferred a quiet dinner with friends. I made these self-negating choices so reflexively that I wasn't even aware that I was making them.*
>
> *This is what many introverts do. It's our loss, for sure, but it's also our colleagues' loss and our communities' loss and – at the risk of sounding grandiose – it's the world's loss. Because when it comes to creativity and to leadership, we need introverts doing what they do best."*
>
> Susan Cain, author of *Quiet: The Power of Introverts In a World That Can't Stop Talking*

Susan Cain defines introversion not as being shy, but being about how you respond to stimulation. Extroverts crave large amounts of stimulation but introverts feel most alive and most capable and switched-on when they are in quieter, more low-key environments.

She says:

> *The key to maximizing our talents is for us all to put ourselves in the zone of stimulation that is right for us.*

That's amazing and useful advice. We don't need to force ourselves into situations that would make us particularly uncomfortable. That would lead us to come across as either a nervous, grumpy wreck, or as false and unauthentic.

HOW NETWORKING AFFECTS YOU:

Networking is important but it doesn't have to be done face-to-face.

The key is not to put on a false cheesy grin and go to a huge writer's conference to do some networking when you'd rather be meditating on top of a mountain.

It's about finding the "zone of stimulation that is right for you", as Susan Cain says in *Quiet*.

cont/d...

Your zone may be:

> ➢ Sitting at a computer sending out press releases and accepting an occasional telephone interview with a reporter.
>
> ➢ Writing a few guest posts for blogs.
>
> ➢ Being a guest on some teleseminars or webinars.
>
> ➢ Starting your own blog and inviting others to write guest posts or do interviews with you.
>
> Networking is about meeting people – that can be virtual or physical. It can be at times to suit you and in ways to suit you. Don't feel you have to hide just because you aren't a party animal.

All these things: Marketing/Advertising, Reputation management, Spinning, Sales, Sending loads of press releases, Telephoning reporters, and Networking can come under the umbrella of PR but PR includes more and more tools as we get more digitally-savvy.

Whether you choose to use any or all of these things is up to you and your level of comfort in how you are prepared to put yourself out there.

You will need to use at least some of the main PR tools:

1. Making relationships with and being available for reporters, the public, and your peers via:

> Press releases – sending to individual reporters/news outlets and distributing online to improve SEO, give backlinks to your website, and boost social proof online.

> Social media – including the main social media platforms: Twitter, Facebook, Google+, LinkedIn, Pinterest; as well as the main book cataloging sites: Goodreads, Shelfari, LibraryThing; and also your website/blog, other people's blogs.

> Newsletters – to people who subscribe to your 'list'. Maintaining an ongoing relationship with your list is one of the most powerful things you can do to boost your book sales.

> Events – such as virtual blog tours, book launch parties, etc. It's important to attend other people's events, as well as your own. Many relationships are made over informal chats when the pressure is off.

> Speaking engagements – offline in libraries, schools, clubs, bookstores, networking events, publishing events; online on podcasts, teleseminars, webinars, YouTube videos, etc.

> Advertising – e.g. Facebook or Goodreads ads, paid book placement on book sites, etc.

> Promotions – competitions of your own, as well as offering a prize in others' competitions.

2. A media kit, consisting of:

- ➢ Your bio.
- ➢ List of FAQ (and answers).
- ➢ A good photograph of you.
- ➢ A list of your books and [possibly] speaking engagements.

Next, we'll look at the skills needed for one of the biggest jobs in PR – writing a press release.

CHAPTER TWO

ANATOMY OF
A PRESS RELEASE

ೞೞ

WRITING A PRESS RELEASE IS AN ART BUT IT is one that can be learned quite quickly. It sounds terribly daunting if you've never written one before but, hopefully, you'll soon be producing them every couple of weeks – depending on how many books you have to promote.

The trick is to not think about writing a press release, but to simply jot down some things about your book and work them up into a release later. These are the things that you will use to make the news of your book **newsworthy** rather than a simple announcement. Editors are looking for news, not corporate backslapping stories.

What's Your Story?

Your news item may be the release of your book on hairstyles for llamas but the story that will get it picked up won't be that – it will be the story **behind** why on earth you're interested in styling llamas' hair, or what goes on in the hills that means llamas need a hairdresser.

It's the same with any book. Pick out something from either the **book** or **yourself** that will interest the news reader. They aren't interested in the fact that you have published a book – that isn't really news, thousands of people publish books every day.

When Michelle wrote her children's novel about a talking dog, she had a couple of news angles that she used in her releases:

> ➢ The dog got the ability to talk thanks to a scientist growing a voicebox for him. This produced a good controversial news item about genetic modification and how far our morals will let us go. (It is also a good topic for talks in schools.)

> ➢ She has a particularly vocal dog herself, who will happily attend interviews to show off his ability to 'talk'. Then she can discuss how awful it would be if dogs could actually speak – humans would never get a word in!

> ➢ She and her illustrator are from the same town, so there was a strong regional theme which a local newspaper picked up on.

It is different for every author and every book. Just remember that the publication of your book isn't news – you have to extract the news from the book itself or from your own story.

The thing that makes something news is that it is:

> **Recent** – if your book about llama hairstyles was published last year that isn't recent. However, if today's headline story is about the decline in the number of people employed as hairdressers, you can write a release about people switching from cutting human hair to cutting animal hair. Pluck something out of the headlines that you can relate to and comment on with some degree of expertise.

> **Important** – news starts with the most important events first, then goes down the list to the less important and the downright trivial. Lots of variations and places for us to get in our story!

> **A first** – odd items will appear on television news because they are firsts. E.g. the first ski-jumping elephant. The first book about llama hairstyles would get attention.

> **Local** – local publications often pick up on stories about local people that national publications would never touch.

> **Unusual** – different things get people's attention.

> **Emotional** – there's a reason why puppy and kitten photos and stories are so popular, they

evoke emotion in us. It's the same with babies, personal tragedy or triumph, and milestones. People can identify with them.

If your book is a novel, you can still pull a story from it. It could be about you, your personal background/experiences, or something based on what your characters go through, the setting, a plot twist, etc.

For non-fiction books, you can produce a 'How To' release, with advice and tips instead of just the fact that your book has been published.

Something to bear in mind is that people want to read things that are of benefit to them – that will increase their earnings, comfort, happiness, health, etc. Have that at the back of your mind when deciding on the story that you can extract from your book or your life.

Keywords

Just as location is important in real estate, keywords are the vital thing with anything that may appear online. Hopefully, you will have done some keyword research before even writing your book – to check that there was a market for it. If not, let's look at the basics.

A keyword can be a single word or a phrase. Choose something that relates to your book or whatever it is you are going to write the release about. Use a keyword tool such as Google's own that comes [free] with an AdWords account or a paid service such as LongTailPro.

That may sound difficult but it isn't. It is just a process of finding out what other people are searching for on Google (and other search engines). That lets you know if the words you have chosen are popular. If they aren't, it is a clue that there may not be a demand for that.

Ideally, use keyword research before even writing your next book, as it will help you get a feel for the potential demand for it.

Most keyword tools will show you what the demand is for the keywords you have entered, and will show you suggestions or other similar, relevant keywords you could try. This is really useful and can give you ideas of things to include in your release.

Using keywords is also known as 'optimizing' your release – or writing it with online distribution in mind. An optimized release is more likely to get published, attract attention, and get clicked on.

So if anyone asks you if you have optimized your release, you can say yes if you have done your keyword research and sprinkled those words throughout the release – including in the headline/title.

It's important to make optimized writing look natural, though. When people first discovered optimization, they wrote what looked like lists of keywords that didn't make any sense! It's still possible to find sites like this, usually ones trying to sell things.

Find your best keywords (you can have several) and build your release around them, rather than trying to cram them into already-written information. Don't repeat them too often, that looks false.

KEYWORD SERVICES

➢ Google AdWords[5] –Google's Keyword Tool used to be a standalone service but now you have to sign up for AdWords. No big deal, it's still free, just takes a few more steps.

➢ Microsoft Advertising Intelligence[6] - downloadable piece of software that is free and useful.

➢ Free Keywords[7] - this is free but you do have to hand over your email address to get access to it (use a sacrificial, free one).

➢ LongTailPro[8] – this has both free and paid levels.

Once you have your keywords you need to ...

Think Of A Short Headline

Start with your headline, based on your keyword research. It should contain your best keyword or keyword phrase and is best kept *short*. This is for a few reasons:

➢ Shorter headlines are more memorable.

➢ Reporters prefer them – they're busy people.

➢ Tweets on Twitter are limited to 140 characters

---

[5] http://adwords.google.com
[6] http://advertise.bingads.microsoft.com/en-us/bing-ads-intelligence
[7] https://freekeywords.wordtracker.com
[8] http://www.longtailpro.com

and you want to be able to tweet your press release headline, if possible.

You can post your press release on your website/blog and then put out a tweet with the headline and the link to the release on your site. Twitter in particular is monitored by reporters, so it is very important when trying to get publicity.

One mistake authors make with their press release headlines is to try to be mysterious with them, thinking that it will make people (reporters in particular) want to read on to find out more. Not a good idea. Reporter turned travel writer Steven Lewis was interviewed[9] by Joanna Penn on *The Creative Penn* podcast. He made this point about headlines:

> *That's a mistake that people sometimes make. They come up with some whimsical, amusing but opaque headline.*
>
> *I'm a journalist, I don't have a lot of time. I might just have time to read the subject-line in my email so if it's something mysterious I'm probably going to hit 'delete'.*
>
> Steven Lewis

In the same podcast, Joanna Penn recommended doing Copyblogger's 'Headline Clinic' to learn how to write

---

[9] http://www.youtube.com/watch?v=RMpoezeLpGI

great headlines. They have a free report[10] – '52 Headline Hacks' – that is very good.

Copyblogger say on their site[11]:

> *On average, 8 out of 10 people will read headline copy, but only 2 out of 10 will read the rest. This is the secret to the power of your title, and why it so highly determines the effectiveness of the entire piece.*

WHAT MAKES A GOOD HEADLINE?

Think about:

> ➢ Emotions - the things that make people *feel* something. What catches your eye when scanning a newspaper? Things that affect you – in terms of safety, finances, health, etc. Shock – people get shocked at different things but using the word 'shock' in the headline will catch a lot of eyes. E.g. 'Shocking statistics about foreign travel', The shocking truth about what's in your water'.

> ➢ Numbers – we love numbers and articles with a number in the title usually get read more than ones without. E.g. 7 Myths About…; 10 Signs

---

[10] http://boostblogtraffic.com/headline-hacks
[11] http://www.copyblogger.com/magnetic-headlines

Your Relationship Needs Help; 3 Reasons You Should Read More.

➢ Reasons – reasons why, how to articles, these catch the eye, especially if they have a short number. E.g. 8 reasons you shouldn't eat xyz; 7 ways to deal with xyz;

Like anything, you will get better at writing headlines over time, with practice. Don't worry if your early headlines aren't wonderful. Even a half-baked press release will still give you extra backlinks to your site, improve your SEO, and give you better social proof. That means that reporters are more likely to find you when they do start looking!

Keep writing press releases, keep working at your headlines, and you'll find them easier to produce and more powerful.

Add Hyperlinks

Hyperlinks, URLs, and web addresses all mean the same thing – a clickable link that will take you somewhere else (it's the basis of the World Wide Web). As press releases are often uploaded in full by press release distribution services, this is very relevant. When you include hyperlinks, it will bring people to your site or wherever you are sending them – perhaps your book's sales page.

If you send them to your website – or, preferably, a special page on your website – you can 'capture' their email address and stay in touch with them.

There's some great advice on Mashable about using hyperlinks in press releases:

> *"I've seen both big and small businesses only link to their product name, which limits the SEO value of your release.*
>
> *Don't put a link to just the product name because, if it's new, there's not a single person who is going to Google that name.*
>
> *Link to a keyword phrase like 'inventory management software' instead, because that's what people are searching for."*
>
> Mark Scott, Gloal PR Manager, NCR

Your book's title may not be keyword-optimized, so don't use that as the hyperlink. Instead, use a keyword that people are likely to search for.

In Word it is quick and easy to create a hyperlink. Simply type a web address in full – starting with *http://* - and then press return on the keyboard. The hyperlink will turn blue and be underlined. It will be 'live' or clickable.

If you want to change it so that the text itself is different to the actual link, here's what to do.

Right-click on the live (i.e. clickable) hyperlink and select EDIT HYPERLINK.

e.g. **http://amazon.com/B0019283**.

In the 'Edit Hyperlink' menu, there will be a 'Text to display' box at the top and an 'Address' at the bottom. Change the text that will show on the page by adding what you want to display in the 'Text to display' box. Leave the 'Address' box the same.

e.g. **llama enthusiasts** would still link to the Amazon page but looks very different.

Not all press release distribution services allow you to do this. Often, they ask for links to be added separately during the upload process. Not to worry, you're still getting great SEO just by having the release out there.

Have Photos Available

You can usually include a photo with a press release. It can be either printed on the page alongside the text, sent as a separate file, or uploaded with the release to the press release distribution site.

We're fortunate, as authors, because we always have a suitable photograph to send with a press release about a new book – the book's cover!

Photos are important because they increase the likelihood of getting your press release published by around **14%**, according to research[12] from PR Newswire and Crowd Factory.

They make you popular with the publication because it means they don't have to send a photographer.

The press release distribution service MyNewsDesk say that including good photos with your press releases increases your chance of publication because:

> *"Picture editors are increasingly having their budgets slashed. This means they're often on the lookout for great photo material. Even bloggers like photos as they strengthen the content of their blog and they often don't have any budget for pictures."*
>
> MyNewsDesk[13]

If your press release is a later story, after the initial one announcing your book's publication, you may need to think of other photographs to send, rather than your cover. You could include both.

You can either get a photographer to take photos for you or take them yourself. Either way, there are a few things to bear in mind:

---

[12] http://www.prnewswire.com/news-releases/press-releases-shared-more-on-facebook-but-twitter-drives-30-percent-more-views-133526808.html

[13] http://insight.mynewsdesk.com/en/tips/increase-chance-publication

- ➤ The best photos convey emotion, or stir up emotion in the people who see them.

- ➤ Go for unusual photos and/or unusual settings. Difference attracts attention.

- ➤ Photos with very simple backgrounds are the most useful. Use a sheet as a background screen if necessary!

- ➤ Add a caption. Again, bear keywords in mind.

IMAGE RESOLUTION

There's a lot of confusion about image resolution, probably because so many things are sent online now. If you are sending something online you generally want it to be as small as possible so it won't use up too much bandwidth and it will send quickly.

However, photos need to be high quality, or high resolution. This is especially important if they may be published in a print publication. They won't generally use photos that are less than 300dpi (dots per inch).

Most modern digital cameras take photos at far greater resolution than 300dpi but many people compress images in order to send them using their regular email software. Gmail, for example, will only send messages of up to 25MB (megabytes). If you want to send a few large photos attached to an email you will soon top that.

Another problem happens when people insert photos directly into their press releases. This isn't a good idea because it makes the photo unusable for the recipient.

That's because Word compresses images without asking for permission!

SENDING PHOTOS

If you are sending your press release directly to a reporter or editor, it is best practice not to include a photo. Instead, put a message on the release that you have high resolution photographs available.

The reason for this is twofold:

> ➢ Images within the press release aren't usable for print publications.

> ➢ Many publications don't accept emails with attachments (which is the most common way to send photos).

If the publication wants to see your photos, they will get in touch to request them. They'll also tell you the best way of sending them to them – they have various ways so there are no right or wrong ways, just specific ways!

If you are using a press release distribution service, check to see what their policies are on photos. It may be that they encourage you to include one on the review itself, or upload it separately.

Either way, stick to their guidelines about the size and/or resolution of your image(s). You can alter them easily in photo editing software such as Photoshop (paid) or GIMP (free), or use an online site such as Pixlr.com.

Starting To Write The Release

Once you have your 'story' or hook – the thing you are going to extract from your book or your own story to work up into a release, you can start thinking about ...

Who, what, when, where, why

These are the 'Five Ws' and were the rule that every person new to PR used to have drummed into them. It's a way to get across the message of the release while you're brainstorming how to write it. Include:

- ➢ Who it is about
- ➢ What happened
- ➢ When it took place
- ➢ Where it happened
- ➢ Why it happened

You may also need to answer HOW it happened in your release.

A press release should consist of:

- ➢ A release date – which tells reporters when the story can be used.
- ➢ A headline – possibly followed by a sub-head.
- ➢ Dateline – the city and state in capital letters, followed by the date.
- ➢ A summary.

➤ The body, usually consisting of:

  ❖ First paragraph – this paragraph could stand on its own if a journalist/editor doesn't have room for the rest of the release.

  ❖ Second paragraph – adds more information.

  ❖ Third paragraph – usually contains a quote or two.

  ❖ [Optional] Fourth paragraph – further information.

➤ A boilerplate – the 'About the author' or author bio.

➤ Contact information.

➤ Links – URLs.

➤ End-of-release marker – 3 hashes, # # #, indicates the end of the release.

We'll look at those in more detail:

RELEASE DATE

It is common practice to put 'For immediate release' or 'For release on ...' with a date.

This is so reporters know exactly when they can write about your story.

HEADLINE

Your headline should be newsy – not just 'new book by ...'. Don't use all capitals, use Title Case. Make sure you get your main keywords in your headline. This is the line you will be tweeting and adding to Facebook,

Google+, etc. You want your keywords everywhere and associated with you and your book.

Avoid any hint of corporate language. Think of people's emotions and needs.

DATELINE

This contains the location and date.

The location is necessary even online. Formats vary but many people put the city and state in capitals, followed by the date in bold.

E.g. [SAN DIEGO, CALIFORNIA] **1st January 2014**

immediately followed by ...

SUMMARY

The summary or lead paragraph goes below the headline and immediately after the dateline. It should be a couple of sentences long and contain the main theme of your release.

It's important not to try to cram everything in here – you want people to want to read on to find out the rest of the story!

What you want in the summary is what you would reply if I asked you what your release was about. Many online distribution sites limit the size of the summary to around 200 characters.

THE BODY

Write the body of your release backwards. The full story needs to be in a nutshell in the first paragraph, then expanded in the following paragraphs. Michelle was always taught that each paragraph – ideally – needs to be able to stand on its own. A busy reporter should be able to cut one or more paragraphs out of your release and it still make sense. That's because different publications have different requirements in terms of length and they may need to pick and choose bits of your release for inclusion.

First paragraph – this needs to expand on your summary. It can even repeat small parts of it. You also need to add a hook, something that gives the main benefit of your book, telling the reader what he/she can get from it. Everybody wants to know "What's in it for me?", this is where you tell them. Otherwise there is no point in them continuing to read it.

The **second paragraph** needs to give a little more background information but, again, this needs to written for the benefit of the reader. People want solutions to their problems, they are not necessarily interested in your expertise or how clever your book is. They want to know what it is going to do for them, how it is going to solve their problem, or make them feel better. Always be thinking in terms of emotional fulfillment.

The **third paragraph** is a good place for a quote from someone relevant – you or another expert. People like a personal touch, a real person talking. You can 'interview' yourself for this. Be sure to do it in the third person – not "I think" but "Belinda the llama hairdresser thinks".

The [optional] **fourth paragraph** can have another quote and some more information to back up the facts that you have already given.

The body should be around 400 words.

BOILERPLATE

The boilerplate is your 'About me' section, or your author bio. Make it short and snappy and something that will be of interest to the reader of *this release*.

So if you write both horror and children's stories, there's no need to go into detail about your horror writing in a release about a children's story. Just a couple of sentences, you don't need to go into too much detail here. Do include a Call-To-Action (CTA) though – e.g. 'Visit 'URL' for more information about ...'.

CONTACT DETAILS

This is for your own or your publisher's name, address, telephone, email.

Sometimes press releases come from publicists, which is why it may not necessarily be your own name. For most authors it is, so don't worry if you are putting your own details here. It is very common for authors to handle some, if not all, of their own publicity, whether they are traditionally published or Indie.

LINKS

Add any links here, even if you have already used them earlier. You might want to add your Amazon author profile page, website, Goodreads author profile page, book sales page, etc.

END OF RELEASE MARKER

The standard market is 3 hashes, separated by spaces - # # #.

Your release should be formatted in single spacing with 6pt after paragraphs on letter size paper. Use a serif font for printed releases, sans serif online (Arial is sans serif; Times New Roman is serif).

Center and embolden the headline and have a space before and after it.

So it should look something like this:

For immediate release (or for release on …)

Headline

Short, snappy. Use keywords – words that people search for.
Author name is not a keyword unless you're Agatha Christie.

[CITY, STATE], *Date* Summary
Get the 5 Ws and How in. Just a couple of sentences.

Paragraph 1

Paragraph 2 Expand on paragraph 1. Sources, quotes.

Paragraph 3 More expansion, another quote.

[Optional] Paragraph 4 Anything you missed?

About/Bio

Contact details

Photographs available (upload if online distribution services allow)

# # #

Links (URLs) can be in the body of the release or uploaded separately on press release distribution sites

Press Release Writing Tips

➤ Firstly, check out other press releases. Use the links in Chapter 9 in this book, Google more, check out published press releases on distribution sites. They can be very inspiring.

➤ Come up with your hook or story about your book, or your background/interests/inspiration for writing the book.

➤ If you haven't already, do some keyword research to find the best keywords. This won't necessarily be your book's genre. It will be about the hook/story.

➤ Be prepared to use different keywords for different press releases. This isn't a one-size-fits-all situation.

➤ Write down the 5 W's and How.

➤ Rough draft your release – not worrying about writing style or press release layout. Write it quickly. Dictate it, if that's easier.

➤ Come up with a good headline – short and snappy. Bear keywords in mind when thinking it up.

➤ Go through the information you have written, rearrange things to look like a press release layout.

➤ Fine tune your message, make sure you have included your most important keywords. Keywords need to be added naturally, as part of the flow of the text.

➢ Make sure you include a quote.

➢ Maintain consistency, especially with keywords – i.e. don't use 'llama hairstyles' in the headline and 'camelid hairstyles' in your summary (for non-llama experts, llamas are part of the camelid family, like dogs are canines!).

➢ Don't write in a passive voice – it sounds too corporate. It needs to sound real and quite fast-paced. Read lots of news articles to get the idea.

➢ Check your spelling and grammar. Then check again. Then get someone else to check. It's so easy to read what you think it says, not what it actually says.

CHAPTER THREE

WHERE TO DISTRIBUTE PRESS RELEASES

CSSO

I N THE OLD DAYS WE PRINTED OUT PRESS releases and sent them manually. Now it's just a click of a button – in theory! In practice it's a little more complicated but there are huge, huge benefits of modern press release distribution because of SEO.

SEO, if you don't already know, is Search Engine Optimization. It's going back to social proof again. Google and other search engines will rank your site, or your book's page on Amazon, higher if they think you're legitimate and not a spam site or a high school kid's first website project.

If they see links to your site coming in from all over the place, they will put you further up the list of results when people search for your key words. Those links will come from your press releases being picked up by online sites that publish them, social media mentions, your LinkedIn profile, and other online places. So the online distribution services are well worth using. They split into the paid and the free, as we'll look at later.

The other places to send press releases are the people who are likely to want to read them, the reporters, other media people, blog owners, and people looking for content for their products. These include:

- Blog owners
- Book reviewers – possibly with an ARC (advance review copy) of your book
- Newspapers
- Magazines
- Radio stations
- TV stations
- Freelance writers
- Researchers

You can buy lists of names or you can compile your own by going to relevant sites online to find contact details. This all takes time and is fine if you have the time but if you don't you could outsource it by going through sites such as PeoplePerHour[14] or Fiverr[15].

There will be people who will research and compile suitable distribution lists for you, and others who will

---

[14] http://www.peopleperhour.com
[15] https://www.fiverr.com

have accounts at the press release distribution services and be able to send your release to them.

Here are some ideas to start with:

➤ Associated Press: *info@ap.org* (Include your press release text in the body of your email, they don't accept attachments.)

➤ US newspapers: *http://www.usnpl.com*

➤ Go to the websites of popular newspapers in your country/region and search for their reporters' contact details. You will often find a list of names and email addresses of editors and reporters responsible for different departments.

➤ Find radio stations, both local, regional, and national: *http://radio.about.com/od/stationdatabases*

➤ Go to a library and ask for media directories.

➤ Google 'press contacts'.

➤ Search on Twitter: 'reporters are covering', the name of particular publications such as 'huffpost'.

MICHELLE'S TOP TIP:

Search top PR agencies on Twitter and look at their contacts. There will be some gold in there! They will have individual press contacts but also check their lists. Often they name them (very helpfully!).

For example, Tangerine PR[16] is one the UK's top agencies. They have lists on their Twitter profile for:

➢ U.K. National journalists

➢ U.K. regional journalists

➢ Freelance hacks for hire

➢ Freelance journalists

➢ And others

Edelman[17] in New York has great lists of reporters on their Twitter account, including:

➢ TIME staff

➢ Newsweek writers

➢ Daily Star reporters

➢ Boston Herald reporters

Find PR agencies that specialize in your genre and look through their lists. They will often be in contact with top reporters and people who book guests for radio and TV shows.

You can subscribe to their contact lists or add some/all of their contacts to your own lists. This will take time but it is time well-spent. Sending one press release to a very relevant reporter can give a better result than sending 200 to reporters who aren't interested in your genre/book.

---

[16] @Tangerine_PR

[17] @EdelmanPR

Now, we're not recommending here that you use Twitter to send your press releases to these reporters and other media contacts. However, if you go to their profiles, you can often find their email address (perhaps after going to their blog or other website).

A bit tedious? Yes, but well worth it. You might consider buying a Fiverr gig and getting someone else to do this for you. Give them a list of PR agencies on Twitter and ask them to go through the contacts' profiles to find email addresses.

It is probably worth following the reporters themselves on Twitter. They can have unique industry insight and break news stories on Twitter that you might want to comment on. Some of them may also follow you back, which could be interesting.

Press Release Distribution Services

A press release distribution service is a bit like the news agencies of old. News agencies gathered news from around the world and sent it out to everyone who had paid to register with them. Reporters would check the 'wire' to see the latest news.

Associated Press and Reuters and examples of news agencies. Initially, the news agencies transmitted their news via telegraphs and some (including Reuters) even via carrier pigeons! They became called 'wire services' because of transmitting via telegraph wires. With developments in technology, the news now comes out via the Internet.

We now have specialist press release distribution services, which not only send regular news but also news sent to them by PR people. The main difference is that press release distribution services don't tend to employ their own reporters but simply gather and send news supplied by others.

They all differ but generally press release distribution services will send releases (online) to search engines, news sites, reporters, and bloggers. Not all will choose to publish your release or follow it up but some will and that's all free publicity and more social proof. Today's newspapers become tomorrow's rubbish but online links last forever.

Every press release you send will be available somewhere online, linking back to your site, giving you social proof, making you easy to find by reporters and others who may be interested in interviewing you.

PAID OR FREE?

There are free press release distribution services. As you get what you pay for, if you use a free service you might have to do a bit of extra work yourself.

Free services generally just SHOW your release, they don't often have a network of reporters to send it out to. Good for SEO and social proof though.

Paid services will usually show your release (often forever) and send it to reporters, editors, bloggers, and anyone else who has signed up to receive specific news items. This makes it more likely to be picked up and appear in print, TV, radio, etc.

Not all distribution services are successful in distributing their information. A study[18] by Vitispr.com into free services revealed that only 5% of them were getting press releases onto Google News; 49% were able to get releases indexed by Google search; and none were effective at getting the information picked up by reporters.

The best free service they found at getting information onto both Google News and Google searches was PR Fire. Others proved to be better at link building (PR Zoom and Idea Marketers). We both rate PRLog highly, it serves us well, is free and effective.

So should you use paid or free? It depends on your budget and what value you put on your time. We use a combination of several free distribution services and manual sending to specific reporters/sites.

Here are some of the top press release distribution services:

PAID SERVICES

PRWEB

This is generally considered to be the best press release distribution service – but it comes at quite a

---

[18] http://www.vitispr.com/blog/free-press-release-sites/

cost. It's a cost that, often, isn't recovered by most authors, especially beginning authors.

Their 'Basic' level costs $99 per release. The release is hosted (permanently) on PRWeb and can be found via search engines. Sometimes news agencies will monitor this as well.

Their 'Standard' level cost $159 per release. It is hosted and sent to news outlets.

Their 'Advanced' level costs $249 per release. For that they submit it to premium news sites, as well as host it, and they also optimize the release.

Their 'Premium' level costs $369 per release. They distribute these to the big guns – New York Times, USA Today, etc. They do this via Associated Press, one of the old-style news agencies. With the premium level, releases can include video and other attachments.

Is it worth it? If you are aiming for a New York Times bestseller then it possibly is worth it – you'll get that money back in no time. However, most of us aren't in that arena and the risk is rather high of not earning enough back to make it worth paying out.

All PRWeb is doing is saving you the time and effort of sending your release out yourself. You can get a similar effect by using a cheaper distribution service or by using a free one and sending releases to individual reporters.

PRESSAT

Pressat is a UK-based service but distributes Internationally via Thomson Reuters. Their all-in-one U.K. package is just £50 (about $85). It's a very targeted service. They decide who to send each press release to, from their lists of local, regional, and national newspapers, online news sites, TV stations, radio stations, trade journals, magazines, and news agencies.

MYNEWSDESK

MyNewsDesk is a bit different. It's a combination of a news service and a PR platform. It was founded by people with 'journalistic and web backgrounds', who wanted to put the 'relations' back into public relations. They wanted to:

"Create a platform that would increase engagement between companies and their most important influencers, such as journalists, bloggers, and other opinion leaders."

They have done this by creating a site which links reporters to the relevant news they need. It doesn't just push the news at them it provides it in a digital newsroom.

There is a 10-day free trial of the Premium service – which costs an eye-watering £5,940 per year (around $10,000). After the 10 days, though, your account reverts to a free one. You can keep it at that or upgrade to one of their other packages.

Check out the pricing packages at:

http://get.mynewsdesk.com/en/price_packaging

FREE SERVICES

You can expect some spam mail if you use a lot of free distribution services. It is worth creating an extra email account specially for publicity purposes. Many sites – such as PRLog – require you to use a company email address rather than one from a free service.

If you have a website it is easy enough to get an email address. If you don't, it is worth buying a domain name in your own author name so you can set up a quick WordPress site and have a couple of email addresses to use.

PRFIRE

This is free but they do have paid packages as well. Free releases need to be well-written and not include images or videos.

http://www.prfire.co.uk

PRZOOM

PRZoom's site looks a bit spammy but is quite effective at link building. Again, they have both free and paid services. Try out the free service before upgrading.

http://www.przoom.com

PRLOG

PRLog distributes to Google News and other search engines. Their free service distributes to search engines and via email and rss, as well as hosting the release on PRLog. They also use social sharing on Facebook and Twitter and, unusually for free services, will include one photo and 3 hyperlinks. It's very good and is the primary service that we use.

www.prlog.org

TOP TIPS FOR USING FREE PRESS RELEASE DISTRIBUTION SERVICES:

➢ If you are linking to an Amazon book page, don't use the short version of the link (the one you can get by clicking on the little envelope icon on the book's page). Many services don't accept redirects, they want the full URL.

➢ They will have different requirements for photo sizes. Check before uploading. If you need to reduce the dimensions or size, use photo editing software, not Word. Pixlr is a free online photo editor: *http://pixlr.com*

➢ Use a sacrificial email account, preferably a 'company name' one rather than a free one. So that would be one that looks like: *yourname@yourwebsite.com* rather than one that looks like: *yourname@hotmail.com*.

➢ Most services limit the number of releases you can send per day. Keep your release in a Word document and put a table at the end of it, on a new page, showing which sites you uploaded it to, with the date, and the link they give you when it has uploaded. You can then send it to individual reporters or whole lists of media contacts, and keep a note in the table of each.

➢ For Amazon rankings, it is best to stagger publicity efforts rather than have everything on one day. So if you write a few releases about one book, don't send them all at the same time. Send one this week and one a week or two later.

➢ Keep thinking up new angles and stories for your releases and send them regularly.

CHAPTER FOUR

MAKING THE MOST OF NEWS OPPORTUNITIES

CஓஒD

YOU MAY NOT THINK YOUR BOOK IS NEWS-worthy but, if you keep an eye on the news, you may spot something that you could use as a 'hook'.

One of the best ways of monitoring news is to sign up for Google Alerts. This is free a service from Google that will send you emails with links to items of interest to you.

They are immensely useful. If you had written the llama hairstyle book, you could set up a few alerts so you would get emails when llamas are mentioned in the news, when animal hairstyles are mentioned, when there are any stories about Peru, wool, or spinning.

Then on the day when a llama with an odd hairstyle makes the news, you can whizz off a press release with your comment about it. Perhaps it could be along the lines of how much a hairstyle affects a person's behavior and this is even more so in animals.

You would link, naturally, to your book in the release but not overtly. You could simply refer to yourself as 'Leading author and llama hairstyle expert Berlinda Rossetti says ..." and then have the Amazon link to your book further down the release.

This will establish you as a leading expert on llama hairstyles and could possibly get you interviews in future. There could be a reporter desperately searching for llama hairstyle experts to get some quotes for a story about the improved employment prospects for hairdressers in Peru. If he Googles 'llama hairstyle expert' your name should come up. He should be able to find you and check your credentials very easily via your website, LinkedIn profile, and other mentions. Once he realizes you're the real deal, he should be able to find your contact information on your website or LinkedIn profile. Hopefully you will have included a telephone number as many reporters still like to be able to pick up the 'phone to get hold of a contact quickly.

Now, there may be other llama hairstyle authors out there (!). Perhaps a few people have spotted a previously untapped niche and have written some quick Kindle eBooks about llama hairstyles. The reporter will probably just find the Amazon links to their books and not much else.

You will appeal to him because you have read this book and understand that you need to be *everywhere* online in order to stand out from the herd. Your LinkedIn profile, in particular, will reassure our roving reporter that you are a legitimate expert, not just someone cashing in on a passing phase.

This has happened to both of us. Michelle is regularly approached in her capacity as an expert on Goodreads, because she wrote a book about it and has guested on numerous webinars, teleseminars, and workshops. Nancy has the dubious honor of being approached regularly not just by reporters but also by traditional publishers because she is seen as an expert in the field of genealogy (dubious because traditional publishing contracts aren't as lucrative as self-publishing!).

Go to *http://www.google.com/alerts* to sign up for Google Alerts. Go to Peru to find out more about llamas. Or Google them, it's cheaper.

Comment On News

An author friend of ours published a health book and wrote a press release about it that she asked Michelle to take a look at. Having read it, it was fresh in Michelle's mind when she was reading an online newspaper the next day. There was an article about health and it was closely related to the content of our friend's book. So Michelle was able to send the link to the article to the author and advise her to get something across to the paper the same day with her own comment, in the form of a press release.

Now, your comment may not be published if you do this but you will have started a conversation with the publication, or with the reporter who reads your comment. They may then approach you in future for a quote about a story. Reporters are always looking for people to give them quotes for stories and they do save the contact details of people who approach them.

The thing about news opportunities is to act *fast*. If you read an article that you could intelligently comment upon in some form of expert capacity, write it out quickly and send it. Not just same day, possibly even same hour. News happens that fast.

You can write your comment as a press release, or as a simple email. Reporters' emails are often listed on media websites and are easy to find.

Keep a note of everything you send to reporters and any coverage you get. A simple spreadsheet is enough. In particular, keep a note of their correspondence with you. An email signature could contain their personal cellphone number and give you a way to contact them later on if they get a job at the New York Times.

Post About News

You don't have to approach the newspaper/magazine directly when you see a relevant news item if you don't want to. You can go to one of your social media platforms to talk about it. Link to the news item's URL and write your comment.

We both do this a lot and it has many benefits:

> It links you with that publication.

> It gets people talking.

> It makes you look current.

> It helps to establish your credibility as an expert on that topic.

Any of the social media platforms are suitable for this sort of 'news comment'. If you post on one, you can link to it on another. So perhaps you have written a book about genetic modification and want to comment on a news story about GMOs.

Blog About News

This is similar to posting on social media except that you post on your own website. You have more control with your own site and can add photos, videos, even an audio comment (just speak into a mic and record it in free software such as Audacity).

Commenting on news stories aligns your site/blog with the site that the news item came from. Be sure to link to that site in your article – perhaps twice.

Just follow a few simple rules:

> Keep polite and professional.

> Don't be negative. You can say something isn't a great thing, just don't phrase it like Eeyore would.

> Get your facts straight. You could be accused of defamation if you repeat an untruth or say

something outrageously bad!

➢ Be very careful if commenting on things that involve court cases – or could lead to a court case. Again, keep to the facts, don't speculate.

Once you have posted the article on your blog, you will have a URL for that post and you can post that URL on your social media platforms.

You can even turn your blog post into a press release: "Llama hairdressing expert causes controversy".

Video About News

You may shudder at the thought of appearing in videos – many people hate the idea. Remember that you don't have to appear on-camera yourself in order to produce successful videos. There are lots of options for videos, including:

➢ Narrated PowerPoint/Keynote presentation.

➢ Animated or 'Handwriting' videos – either using paid software such as EasySketchPro[19], VideoScribe[20], PowToon[21] or doing it manually[22].

➢ MovieMaker compilation using photographs (check copyright) or other images, with you narrating.

---

[19] http://easysketchpro.com
[20] http://www.sparkol.com/products/videoscribe
[21] http://www.powtoon.com
[22] Useful free tutorial: ttp://www.youtube.com/watch?v=YxW5FfuFyvc

YouTube has amazing SEO benefits. Make the most of them by filling out the description of your video with lots of keywords and the link to your website, book, press release, etc.

Do A Hangout Discussion

If something big is going on in the news and you have some sort of expert status on that topic, you might want to create a Hangout to discuss it.

Google Hangouts can be joined by anyone with a Google+ account. You can choose an ordinary hangout or Hangouts On Air, which streams live on YouTube and Google+ at the time of the hangout.

You could do your own hangout and read out a list of questions that you can answer, or invite people to join you to discuss the trending news item.

CRBO

The big thing to remember about news stories is that you have to act quickly. An item at the top of yesterdays news may have completely disappeared from today's, or at least be wallowing at the bottom of the list and be considered too unimportant to pick up and run with again.

If you can comment quickly enough, you stand a chance of joining in the news at the time.

You can still comment afterwards, in blogs, videos, etc., and that will be great for you SEO. If you want to be picked up by some of the big guys, though – radio and TV in particular – you need to move fast.

If something on the morning news is relevant to you:

> Pick up the telephone, call the newsdesk and ask if they would like to interview you.

> Send an email to the reporter who broke the story, offering your comment on any follow-up he/she does. (Check out the station's website for contact details. If none are listed, telephone the station and charm the receptionist into giving up the email address!)

> Put a press release together containing your comment on the item and send it to other news outlets – they often pick up on stories that 'bigger' rivals have run.

> Check the station's website for a link to submit news items. This has worked for Michelle – she received a telephone call an hour later from an interested reporter looking for a filler story. In the end, his larger story fell through and she ended up with a much bigger slot.

CHAPTER FIVE

MEDIA TRAINING 101

 CS&O

MICHELLE WAS TEACHING I.T. TO A CLASS OF teenagers when the school administrator dashed into the room with a portable telephone. He said it was a very insistent researcher from a BBC regional radio station, wanting to speak to her urgently.

She took the call, with an audience of students who suddenly became terrific listeners for the first time that term. The researcher explained that a guest had let them down at the last minute and they needed a replacement. This was when Michelle was combining teaching at school with running a training center. The station needed her to speak about training in the 21st century. She was pleased with the opportunity but had no time to prepare herself – the slot was due to start in 10 minutes.

She did her first radio interview in 20 years while pacing around the courtyard of the school, trying to keep warm. Not the most ideal circumstances but it shows how quickly you can be called on if you send out press releases!

When she got back to the classroom, it was to a round of applause – the tech-savvy teens had listened in to the station online. Not only that, they had had the presence of mind to download a piece of software to record the interview for her. So she was able to save the recording to her website and blast it out on social media.

She would like to think that she had taught those kids well but, actually, their generation are naturally good at things like that. They have been brought up with the Internet, with fast-paced games, and the whole celebrity culture. We tend to see that as a bad thing but it has made them very adaptable and capable in the technological age.

For those of us who grew up with nothing more gadgety than Lego™, responding quickly and being tech-savvy isn't natural, it's learnt. We've included a quick media training primer here but please bear in mind that we aren't media trainers. This is fine if you have a quick telephone interview with a reporter who has received your press release. You definitely need more training if you are going to appear on TV or if you think you may have a controversial topic to deal with. You can easily turn a media interview into a PR nightmare if you go in too naïve and trusting.

One of the best media trainers in the business is Brad Phillips, who runs the MrMediaTraining[23] website. It's a fantastic site, full of helpful articles and tips.

Reading some media training advice would put you off ever agreeing to an interview with a reporter! Don't panic, mostly they are just looking for some half-decent copy to meet their deadline. Unless you are embroiled in a political scandal or up to something dodgy, there isn't going to be much for them to unearth that could worry you.

Big time media training is for PR professionals and company spokespeople. They often have to deal with reporters enquiring about forthcoming but confidential employee lay-offs, whether their company is involved in third-world exploitation, what their CEO has been up to, etc. Difficult things to handle. Knowing what to say and what not to say, and how you present yourself, if really important.

Most authors won't come across anything more difficult than trying to remember the date we published our book, if we're asked.

Dealing With Questions

Go in forearmed. Hopefully you will have built up a file (physical or digital – Evernote is handy if you prefer digital) of things the press may be interested in. You should also have a page on your website full of relevant information that you can direct reporters to.

---

[23] www.mrmediatraining.com

You'll need the titles of your books, when they were published, where they are for sale, and a story about each of them. You'll also need your own background story, your inspiration for writing, little bits of personal information that you're willing to share publicly (hobbies, where you're from, a little family information such as number of children, your writing day, etc.).

All media trainers will tell you never to say "No comment" in answer to a question from a reporter. It's like dangling a bone in front of a hungry dog. Instead, be honest and say you aren't able to give them an answer to that but you can say … and give them something else. Politicians are excellent at this.

You also need to be aware that a reporter won't just report on what you tell him/her when the camera or microphone is running. Everything you say to them, at any time and in any format, could be used in their report. Too many people have been caught out by having a friendly talk with a reporter after he's switched his microphone off, only to find their informal chat becoming the headline of the story.

In our experience, local and regional interviews are *generally* pleasant and non-confrontational. If you have the possibility of a national interview and are even slightly concerned about how to handle it, get some advice from a media trainer.

Being A Good Guest

If you are a guest on a radio or TV show, Google Hangout, webinar, or YouTube video, there are a few things to bear in mind:

➢ Ask how long they would like your answers to be. Some interviewers like to ask one or two questions and have their guest speak for the rest of the time. Others (especially radio and TV hosts) prefer 30-second answers. Deadlines are tighter in traditional media than online.

➢ Ask if there are any topics they would like you to stay away from, or to concentrate on.

➢ 'Arrive' early (even online) – leave extra time for travelling, just in case. With online interviews, log in early, having tested your equipment first.

➢ Turn off your cellphone/tablet and any desktop notifications on your computer, for online interviews.

➢ If you have anything to show on-camera, ask the crew first. It may not be allowed. If it is, they know best how to show it and will advise you how and where to hold it.

➢ Be aware that you may still be appearing on-screen or may still be heard, even when you aren't answering a question.

➢ Don't fiddle with clothes, hair, or rings.

➢ Keep hand and head gestures under control.

➢ Don't interrupt (viewers/listeners hate it and so

do the editing staff).

➤ Don't refer to an earlier comment – it may be deleted in the edit.

➤ Don't swear – ever. Marie Forleo's earliest interviews – when she didn't have a large audience - often included mild swearing but it's interesting that she's cut that out now she's super-successful. It alienates.

➤ Stay in your seat after the interview. Allow them to unclip you, tell you you're good to go, etc., so you don't interrupt the next piece on air.

Appearance

One of the most impressive author celebrities of the moment is Marie Forleo[24]. She has a huge following for her YouTube videos and business training. When she started out, her videos looked quite home-made. It's really interesting to compare her old videos with her latest ones. Now, she has a team, a stylist, a professional studio, and planned scripts. She's good to watch for ideas on appearance, style, and content.

In her earliest videos – from 2010 – she is seen in a very domestic environment, with her hair loose and unglossed, minimal makeup, and she is dressed down, frequently in shorts and t-shirts. Compare that to her new videos, where she looks like she's ready for the red carpet at the Oscars.

---

[24] http://www.youtube.com/user/marieforleo

The point to get here is that she got successful anyway, even when she was dressed down and using [we guess] a regular camcorder. Do your best with your appearance but don't stress about it. The best way to look good is to feel confident. If you are at your best in baggy jeans and sweater, then go with that look. As authors, we are allowed – even expected – to be a little bohemian.

It's more important to find your own look so that you are relaxed and confident than to try to emulate someone else. You won't be happy in their skins.

One of the best things you can do is to get your colors done – or to wear your colors if you have had them done and aren't following the guidelines! Be sure to tell the color expert that you are going to appear on-camera as they will know the best colors for that.

We have found that this works particularly well for men. They have so little choice (compared to women) about their appearance, especially in formal situations. The choice is which suit and which shirt and tie, very limited. If you're a guy, getting your colors done can give you a huge boost as you'll be wearing colors that make you look and feel great.

Women, too, can go from feeling okay to feeling amazing, just by careful color selection.

Michelle had her colors done years ago. She had felt that she was born too late and would have preferred to be a 60s flower child. She has long, curly hair and favors natural fabrics and colors. They don't favor her, though! They make her look washed out and too 'country' for business occasions.

She now knows that her bold, confident colors are deep and jewel-like. She only has to put on her tomato red top or a vibrant blue dress to feel businesslike, confident, and ready for anything. Unfortunately, those jewel colors aren't always the best for appearing on-camera and she has to tone it down to more muted tones. There's a big psychological lift with colors that goes deeper than knowing you look good.

Tips For Appearing On Camera

Dressing for appearing on-camera used to only apply to authors who were going to be interviewed on TV. Now it applies to a large number of us because we are often called on to be interviewed in webinars, Google Hangouts, YouTube videos, etc. There are a few things we need to be aware of, just like the TV pro's of old:

- ➢ Avoid busy patterns and fabrics, e.g. checks, stripes, herringbone. They can create a wavy effect onscreen, making viewers think their eyes are going gozzy! Solid colors are better.

- ➢ Wear your best colors near your face:

  - ❖ Blue looks good on-camera. Green can look odd.

  - ❖ Pastels can be good but white can go weird on-camera, giving off a slight glow that can be very distracting.

  - ❖ Red doesn't always work well onscreen, as it

can 'bleed' and make you look flushed.

➢ Keep jewelry minimal and understated. Certainly don't wear anything that makes a noise, it's surprising how noisy it can be when picked up by a microphone.

➢ Specifically for men: if you're going to wear a suit, make it a light one rather than a funereal black. Shirt cuffs should show about 1" beneath jacket sleeves. Unbutton the bottom button of your jacket if you're going to be sitting down, so it won't bunch up. You might not want to wear makeup but if you don't you're in danger of shiny face. A light dusting of powder can prevent that and keep you looking cool and professional. Don't be tempted to try talcum powder – you could look like a ghost! If you have any bald spots on your head, powder those too.

➢ Specifically for women: be careful with skirt lengths if there's any chance of your legs appearing on-camera. If you reveal too much leg it can detract from your message at best and unleash a PR nightmare at worst. Do wear makeup, even if you don't usually. As with men, a slightly matte finish is good. Not a dull matte, just not shiny. Avoid glittery/shimmery makeup. Do your eyes with a good mascara and a light liner at the outer thirds of the eyelid. Don't go for an Egyptian look with smoky eyes. It can look over-done and can run. If you wear glasses for reading, they can magnify your eyes and that, combined with over-done eye makeup, can be a disaster!

➢ Hair: make sure it's neat and not fly-away. All the electrical equipment can cause it to stand on end! A quick flick over with a dryer sheet can take the static away. If you have a choice with your hairstyle, choose to keep it an inch or two away from your eyes – or it can cause shadows.

➢ Glasses: if you wear them, an old trick Michelle was taught by a reporter was to always get anti-glare treatment on them when you get a new pair and to wear them slightly tipped forward. This reduces glare. (Michelle got so used to this that she still wears glasses with the arms slightly above her ears!)

➢ Check your appearance in a well-lit mirror before the interview. Look out for any specks of dandruff on your shoulders, lipstick on your teeth or cabbage between them, running makeup, shiny forehead, or other distractions.

➢ Get your energy up before the interview so you don't come across as flat and low-energy. Psyche yourself up, do a couple of press-ups or squats, do a victory punch – it all helps to get your in a good state of mind, get the blood flowing, increase your oxygen, and get a fighting spirit.

➢ Be careful with elaborate hand gestures and other physical habits. If you're a toe tapper, that could be picked up on the microphone. If you speak with your hands, you could be in danger of knocking the camera over! Don't think you have to sit on your hands, though, some hand gestures can be effective.

> Lean slightly forwards towards the camera. It seems natural, more energetic, and less stiff.

> Keep still if you're on Skype or Google Hangouts – people with low bandwidth will see you as jumpy otherwise.

> Don't use 'er', 'um', and other vocal ticks. Poor Caroline Kennedy was lambasted in the press for repeating "you know" so much in interviews. In fact, some people believe that this unfortunate verbal problem cost her a senate place. The New York Daily News[25] were particularly scathing about her TV performances (where she repeated "you know" 130 times in one interview) and asked a voice coach about them. She said:

> *"She's just inexperienced. It's just a habit, the way young people all say 'like' every other word. I don't think she even knows she's doing it, to that degree."*
>
> Jocelyn Rasmussen[26], voice coach

Quite. So we need to ask our loved ones and our not-so-loved ones to let us know if we have a problem. If you do, start training yourself out of it. Record yourself talking, imaging that you

---

[25] http://www.nydailynews.com/news/politics/caroline-kennedy-whiz-words-article-1.355586

[26] http://www.jocelynrasmussen.com

were being interviewed, or get a friend to interview and record you over Skype. There's nothing like watching yourself afterwards to snap you out of verbal ticks!

Technical Tips

➢ Get to know the technology before you use it. If you have an interviewed planned using Skype or Google Hangouts, try the software before so you know how to use it. With hangouts, you will need to be in the circle of the person who is running the hangout. If that's you, make sure all the people you want to participate are in your circles.

➢ Mute your microphone if you need to cough or if a household noise happens, such as a barking dog.

➢ Use ear buds rather than speakers to reduce feedback and echo.

➢ If possible, have equipment available in case of problems. So you might be set up with a webcam and laptop – if you also have an iPad, have that nearby so you can switch to it in case the laptop develops a fault.

➢ A good webcam will often make you look better than an embedded one that comes with a laptop. The camera on the modern iPad is very good.

➢ If possible, don't have the camera/webcam low down on the desk. It can accentuate a double-chin, and even make it look like you have one when you don't. It's better at eye-level or slightly above.

➢ Be careful where you're looking. Looking at your

computer screen seems natural – and polite, as you're looking at the person who is talking to you. But that will probably mean that you aren't looking at the camera. So you could look slightly shifty! Try to remember to look at the *camera*.

➤ If you need a microphone, get a good one. The iRig HD is the one we recommend. The Blue Yeti is also good. Have the mic on a stand rather than on the desk, where it could pick up computer vibrations and the sound of the fan. If you can't afford or don't have space for a stand, you can put the mic in a block of foam as the foam will absorb vibrations so the mic doesn't pick up on them.

➤ Position the mic a hands' width away from your mouth and use a pop filter[27] – an inexpensive device that sits in front of a mic. Here's how to put the mic exactly where it should be:

> *Make a fist and stick your thumb and pinky out. Put your thumb on your lips and position the mic so it is just touching your pinky. Then put the pop filter in front of it.*
>
> *This reduces the 'pop' noise when you say certain consonants. This distance is near enough to get good sound levels but far enough away to avoid distortion.*

[27] http://amzn.com/B008AOH1O6

➢ Do get a pop filter for your mic – or make one from a piece of wire and a piece of pantyhose. It makes a huge difference and can make an inexpensive mic sound like a top dollar one.

➢ Have everything charged up that needs charging. We've actually heard guests on webinars apologize and have to go off and look for their laptop charger!

➢ Keep your desk clear and switch off other gadgets so you aren't distracted.

➢ Turn off all desktop notifications on the computer you'll be using – e.g. antivirus, Dropbox, Windows Update, etc.

➢ Think about what's behind you. If the room doesn't look good, put up a sheet behind you as a backdrop. It makes you look better and stand out more. Blue is the best color for this – think of White House press briefings. Or try to find a corner of your house that looks great – perhaps of a bookcase containing your books! Move things into shot to make it look better: a plant or a vase of flowers. You could even put a poster on the wall of something related to your profession.

➢ Have a light – preferably two – in front of you, in front of the camera/webcam. Certainly don't have lights behind you, even a window.

Tips For Running Your Own Interviews

It can be very good publicity for yourself and your books to conduct your own interviews. You can post these on YouTube and embed them on your website/blog, Goodreads profile, Amazon author central, etc.

You could interview other authors, your fans, industry professionals, etc.

The same rules apply with regards to appearance and technical issues. There are a few extras, too:

➢ Google Hangouts On Air are great for doing a live interview, which will appear on YouTube and Google+. These are recorded automatically but the quality isn't always the best. Consider running other software on your computer to record the event – Screenflow (Mac) or Camtasia (Windows & Mac) are the best.

➢ Ask guests to turn off desktop notifications on their computers/devices.

➢ Suggest that they mute their microphones when they aren't talking – this is especially important in a group chat.

➢ Give guests the time of the interview well in advance and send reminders the day before.

➢ Check that they have used the software before, run through it with them if not.

➢ Be careful to only ask one question at a time. That

may sound obvious but it is surprising how many people ask a question and then go straight on to ask another, expecting the guest to remember both questions when answering. They could be feeling slightly nervous and under pressure, memory goes out of the window when under stress.

➢ Be very careful not to talk when someone else is talking and ask that you guests do the same.

➢ Open and close the interview with thanks to your guests and follow-up with social media thanks as well.

➢ Be sure to have a call-to-action in your interview and in the description of it. Include links to your guests' websites/Amazon pages, your own, and any books that the interview relates to.

➢ Consider doing a regular interview and turning it into a podcast. This can raise your profile and help you make great connections.

Finally, don't forget your plug, your call-to-action. It may not always be possible to get in everything you want to say, but you need to at least give your website URL or mention that your books can be found on Amazon.

CHAPTER SIX

THE PR POSSIBILITIES OF SOCIAL MEDIA

ⓒⴺ𐭀

HAVE YOU EVER MET A DINOSAUR – OR ARE you one yourself?! The Internet definition of a dinosaur is not a scaly beast with tiny arms and a penchant for appearing in blockbuster movies. It is:

> *A person or thing that is outdated or has become obsolete because of failure to adapt to changing circumstances.*

If you have been avoiding social media you may be in danger of becoming a dinosaur. It might seem frivolous, a waste of time, tedious, or overwhelming – and it can be all of those things! - but social media is an enormously important part of the marketing mix that you ignore to your cost. We mean that literally – it will cost you in the loss of potential royalties.

Social media platforms are simply websites that allow people to communicate informally with others – via written messages, photos, audio, or video. It's the online equivalent of chatting over the garden fence, or in the town square. It is still about being social and making time for people. Those who won't chat, who don't make time for others are never heard. Their message (in our case about our books) might be wonderful but there's no-one to hear it. If you don't have time for your potential readers, you don't have time for your readers – they'll pick up on that.

In the 20th century, 'Whodunit' books were very popular – think Agatha Christie's 66 detective novels. The entire book would be about trying to guess who the murderer was. Those type of books aren't the norm now. The modern version of a Whodunit is more of a Whydunit. Readers want psychological insight into the murder's mind, his motivations, his background, what led him to commit his dreadful act.

Not only do readers want to know the characters in their novels in a deeper way, they want to know their favorite authors as well. They want to feel that they know more about why you wrote, what inspires you, what makes you tick. You don't have to give them too much personal information, of course, just enough to make them feel you are being open and honest.

Why You Need To Be On Social Media

The world is on social media. News stories are frequently reported on Twitter long before the traditional reporters and broadcasters have picked up on them. In fact, many reporters will tell you that they spend more time on Twitter than any other social media platform. Twitter is very fast-moving and the messages (tweets) are short – limited 140 characters. That fits in with the reporting lifestyle. Life in a newsroom is very fast, with lots of noise and things going on at once. So we know that Twitter is the place to be if you want to stand a chance of catching a reporter's eye. There are others as well, though, that are worth giving some consideration – for lots of reasons.

You may still think you don't want to bother with social media and that's fine but it will greatly hamper your publicity efforts. It makes publicity quick, easy, and *free*.

When Michelle wrote press releases in the past, they were printed, put in envelopes, and physically mailed out to hundreds of reporters and editors. Most of them would end up in the editor's trashcan; only a few would find their way into newspapers, magazines, and radio/TV news or features. It cost money – paper, envelopes, labels, stamps.

Now you write a press release about your book and send it via an online press release distribution service. The distribution service sends it to the major search engines and – possibly – other services, and stores it online. So your press release has a web address, or URL. You can then 'ping' that URL all over the place so that the search engines get double the proof that it exists and isn't just a bit of spam, and they actually 'index' it. That means that you can find it if you search Google for it.

You don't stop there, though. You tweet it, Facebook it, post it on Google+, post a picture of it on Pinterest. Then other people pick up on it and post it to their contacts.

Soon you see the sales of your books start to climb. If you communicate with your readers outside of your book – via a website/blog or on social media – you will discover that they found your book in many different ways. Some from browsing on Amazon, some from a friend's review on Goodreads, others from noticing a tweet on Twitter, others from extract you posted from your book (or your press release) on Google+.

Billions of people are on social media – over a billion on Facebook alone (11% of the entire world!). You have a way of reaching those people that doesn't cost and doesn't take up a whole lot of time.

Why wouldn't you want to be on social media if that is its power? The ability to put your message out there to billions of people is an incredible opportunity. It doesn't bear thinking about what that would cost if you were to buy it in advertisements!

Your 'message' is what you choose to put there as an author 'brand': your interests, likes and dislikes, your writing inspiration, your books themselves, and your journey.

Having a presence across the range of the big social media platforms means that you appear:

- ➢ Accessible – reporters love that, it makes their life easier!

- ➢ Up-to-date – the Internet is constantly changing. Being on social media shows you as being modern and approachable.

- ➢ In demand – successful authors have to have social media profiles to manage all the fan questions and requests. So do you!

Like many things in PR, social media is a long game. You aren't going to sell 1,000 books overnight just because you got 1,000 social media followers or YouTube views. Use social media as a tool to build up your reputation and increase your visibility, not as a 'book blast'.

Get Social Proof

'Social proof' is the new buzz phrase. It's what a lot of people do when they meet someone – check to see if they can find them online. If you are establishing yourself as an expert if you're a non-fiction author, or as an author brand if you're a novelist, then you need to have some 'presence' online so you can be found when people look you up.

In the old, early Internet days, it used to take Google and other search engines weeks to 'find' a website and index it – i.e. make it available when people search for it. Now you can put up a piece of content (e.g. a press release, article, or video) and Google will have it indexed within an hour. That's if you use a Google-owned platform such as Google+ or YouTube but even non-Google platforms are indexed within a couple of days at most.

The potential of this for new authors, especially, is massive. You can establish yourself all over the place within a matter of days, and it will look like you're been around for years.

The beauty of it all is that you don't have to be an extrovert to take full advantage of any of these platforms. You can do it all from the comfort of your desk.

The Big Six Social Media Sites

The most important social media platforms – in terms of number of users, frequency of use, quality of content, and power of social proof are:

- ➤ LinkedIn – http://www.linkedin.com | 300 million users.
- ➤ Twitter – http://twitter.com | 645 million users.
- ➤ Facebook – http://www.facebook.com | 1.35

billion users.

> Google+ - https://plus.google.com/ | 540 million users.

> Pinterest – http://www.pinterest.com | 70 million users.

> YouTube – http://www.youtube.com | 1 billion users.

Having up-to-date profiles on several of these social media platforms, and posting regular messages and conversations with others are becoming increasingly important. It means you 'check out' when you're looked up. You're the real deal!

It isn't necessary to waste hours on social media. If you have a marketing strategy, you'll have it all mapped out how long you spend on the best platforms for you. You'll just need to decide which ones to focus on – we would recommend sticking to just 2 where you will spend most of your social media time. You can also make use of apps and linking so posting on one site will make your material appear on others.

We'll look at the big 6 in more detail and cover a few things that you could do to maximize your use of social media time. Later on we'll look at book cataloging sites that are also worthy of your time and can be added to your marketing mix.

Firstly, some golden rules – things that are common to all social media platforms.

Social Media Rules

Forget old-style broadcasting. Modern publicity involves engagement. People don't know you and will struggle to come across your books on Amazon or other sales sites because there are simply so many books on there. You need to help potential readers get to know and like you – and, ultimately, trust you.

Social media expert John Colley[28] produces excellent courses on Udemy and elsewhere about engaging with your public on social media. He says:

> *"You need to give before you get.*
> *Build relationships before you sell.*
> *This is the inverse of the*
> *traditional way of marketing."*
>
> John Colley

That's what you need to focus on – building relationships. You're going to connect with people by:

- ➢ 'Friending' them on Facebook or getting 'likes' on your page.
- ➢ Adding them to your circles on Google+.
- ➢ Making a first level connection with them on LinkedIn.
- ➢ Following them and having them (hopefully) follow you on Twitter.

---

[28] https://www.udemy.com/u/johncolley

> ➤ Following them on Pinterest and repining their pins.

> ➤ Gaining subscribers on YouTube, commenting, and responding to others' comments.

If that sounds daunting, don't worry, you don't have to do all of it. Just concentrate on one initially and maybe increase to two if it works/you have time/can be bothered. We suspect that you will be sure to make time for social media once you start to reap some rewards from it.

Here are the golden rules:

> ➤ Follow the 80/20 rule – make 80% of your content about others and only 20% about yourself/your books.

> ➤ Don't try to sell. It's fine to post offers – Amazon free days, Smashwords coupons – but don't post "Buy my book".

> ➤ Offer value – your time/expertise/sympathy.

> ➤ Be professional. Use the same good head shot of yourself on each of the social media platforms that you use. You are your brand, not your book, your dog, or your sports team.

> ➤ Create your own content and re-use others' (with attribution – it makes for more relationships).

> ➤ Use a variety of content: text, images, photos, audio, video, presentations (PowerPoint/Keynote). Mix it up, keep it fresh.

> ➤ Re-use your old content: blog posts, press releases, early cover designs.

➢ Respond to comments in a timely way – not 3 months later.

➢ Don't be drawn in by negative people. Remain polite, don't argue.

➢ Refer back to your website – what John Colley refers to as your 'hub'. You can have your website's URL on your press releases, social media profiles, stamped on videos, etc.

➢ Include a 'Call To Action' if possible. People don't tend to take action unless you tell them to – often, they don't realize it is possible/necessary. A simple "Click here to find out more" or "Please share this video" is enough.

➢ Never, ever, ever post, comment, or engage on social media if you are drunk, depressed, or feeling ill.

Above all, always remember the 'social' part of social media – it's about building relationships, not about broadcasting about yourself or your books.

Twitter

Twitter is great because reporters are on there looking for news and trends. You can post news about your book releases, promotions, signings, etc., as well as comment on news and trends, chat with readers and other authors, and add personal posts so readers feel they are getting to know you. Give readers and potential readers a glimpse into your likes and dislikes - just don't air your dirty washing!

> **Nancy says ...**
>
> *I've been a Twitter user for more than six years, after receiving an invitation from co-founder Biz Stone.*
>
> *I embrace Twitter the same way Michelle embraces Facebook and LinkedIn, probably because I enjoy writing short form, so the 140 character limitation suits my natural writing style.*

Although we could write a book about Twitter (and we may!), there are two things you need to understand about this network:

1. This isn't a place to constantly spam people about your book. Annoying.

2. This is a place to share great articles you've found or written or to answer questions of other Twitter users.

Twitter relationships make a difference in your marketing success. If someone follows you, go to their Twitter profile, read it, and thank them personally. You can always find something in their profile or on their website that you can connect with, so it's easy to thank them with a tweet a bit like this:

Thanks for the follow. I love Scotland too but right now the weather is too wild for me to even think about visiting!

or

Thanks for the follow. The article you wrote on your blog about XYZ was excellent.

or

Thanks for the follow-I see you live in Portland. I used to live in NW – but now that it's the 'Pearl', I probably would be in NE!

If you thank someone personally for following you, you will probably get a response back. Now the two of you are building a relationship. And, from relationships, mutually beneficial projects or shares grow.

The industry buzz is that Twitter has realized how important it is to media professionals and has a new news platform app launching soon.

HOW TO MAKE THE MOST OF TWITTER

- ➢ Create a **profile** for yourself. Include a link to your website/blog, a photo, and some cover art. If you aren't a Photoshop whizz, you can get cover art made cheaply on Fiverr (**http://fiverrcom**).

- ➢ Browse the site regularly and click '**ReTweet**' (known as RTs) on posts that interest you and/or that you think will be of interest to your peers, readers, and/or potential readers.

- ➢ Click '**Reply**' to some tweets, engage in conversation.

- ➢ Set up an **automatic 'direct message'** (i.e. a private message, sent directly to one person. You can send direct messages – DMs – to people you are connected with). Your automatic DM should go to anyone who follows you. Ideally, include a URL to a page on your website where you give something away in return for their email address. This will help you build a 'list' – a collection of email addresses. You can then write to them later – perhaps to ask for beta readers or early reviewers for your next book. SocialOomph is a good service to use for setting up an automatic direct message (**https://www.socialoomph.com**).

➢ Post your own **tweets**: a short message about your day, your writing process, your progress on your current book. Gather things of interest from around the Internet to post and from Google Alerts. Tweets need to 140 characters or less. If you use up the 140 characters, you make it harder for people to RT your tweets, so try to keep them well below the limit. If you want to RT someone else's tweet but it won't fit within the 140 character allowance, you can cut it down a little but add MT (= Modified Tweet) to indicate this.

➢ Add *images* when you can. Even on Twitter, images are important.

➢ Use **hashtags**. These are topics that you precede with a hash (#) symbol. The hash turns the topic into a clickable link. People can click on the hashtag links and see all the tweets that use that hashtag. Hashtags were first used on Twitter but are now used on other platforms – with varying degrees of success, they are pretty much hated on Facebook. They make Twitter very special, though, as it's a great way for people to search for topics that interest them. For this reason, don't use overly-long or obscure hashtags that no-one is going to be searching for and that will use up most of your 140 character allowance! Hashtags are a bit over-used, keep to a maximum of 2 or 3 per tweet.

➢ Use **mentions**. If you precede someone's Twitter name (their Twitter 'handle') with an '@' symbol, it will make your tweet appear to that person's followers (as well as your own). It's a good way to get your Twitter profile in front of people who don't follow you. It's also a good way to start a conversation.

As part of our research for this book, Michelle studied a Udemy course by social media marketing experts Chris Wilkey and Austin Hostetter, 'Creating Effective Social Media Content for Business Use'. In it, they point out that starting a tweet with an '@' symbol and a person's Twitter handle will make that tweet only appear to your own and that person's followers.

That's not always what you want if you are trying to increase your reach.

Here's what to do:

> ***You can put a period (.) in front of the '@' mention to stop Twitter only sending that tweet to yours and the person's followers.***
>
> Austin Hostetter, Digital Media Expert

Genius!

While we are on the genius of Chris and Austin, they also recommend that you don't link your Facebook and Twitter accounts. This is possible and may seem like a good idea because you only have to post once and it will appear on both platforms. However, there are a couple of reasons why this isn't a good idea.

> ➢ As we mentioned, the Facebook community still has a dislike of hashtags.

> ➢ Twitter is a much faster-paced, newsy community, where things can be repeated several times over the course of a day.

> ➢ Tweets are often part of a conversation and, while your tweets will be sent to your Facebook profile, the other person's tweets won't be. So your Facebook friends will wonder what on earth you are talking about.

It is safer to link your Facebook and Goodreads accounts, which we'll look at later.

Facebook

Once the domain of teenagers and their zit problems, Facebook has become a force to be reckoned with for businesses and brands, with many of them using it successfully.

It is useful for authors because you can have a private profile and a public page. So you can keep your profile for friends and family if you wish but establish a business page for yourself as an author and a page for each book or genre/series.

Having a page means that advertising on Facebook is easier as you can direct people who click on ads right to your page (or a tab linked from your page). This is cheaper than sending people to an external website such as Amazon.

We are both fans but Guy Kawasaki, author of A.P.E., isn't. He says:

> *Facebook is for people you already know ... your existing social graph. It's great for reaching them.*
>
> Guy Kawasaki

Kawasaki believes that Facebook is limited in its effectiveness for book marketing because we tend to use it to engage with existing friends, family, ex-colleagues, etc. He feels that if they aren't in our target market, then we are wasting our efforts.

That may be just him, though. Plenty of authors we know personally and virtually have harnessed the power of Facebook with great success. Don't underestimate the power of Facebook. 'Only' telling your trusted friends, family, and colleagues about your book can be a very good way of getting early reviews and interest in it. Many people connect with others on Facebook via groups – people they have never met in real life. We both met in a Facebook group and have connected with many other authors, readers, and potential readers.

Michelle says ...

I embraced Facebook after being commissioned to write a training course for businesses on how to use social media. I realized the potential of Facebook and started using it for my own [training] business – the result was more clients and more writing assignments.

I like the fact that Facebook allows for longer content, together with embedded images and videos. Being able to create pages is a huge boon, as it keeps your business and personal activities separate.

If you don't like the fast pace or short, repeated message of Twitter, you may prefer Facebook. You can post videos and images and they will be embedded right on the page.

Pages are a great way to reach readers. You could create a page for each of your books (or book series) and have the URL listed in the book. It gives readers a way to connect with you, find out more about you and your inspiration for writing, perhaps background information on the characters in your book, or extra tips and guides if you are a non-fiction author.

HOW TO MAKE THE MOST OF FACEBOOK

- ➤ Set up a Facebook **profile**. Include the address of your website/blog, if you have one.

- ➤ Set up a **Goodreads** account (more on that later) and link it to your Facebook account.

- ➤ Create a Facebook **page** for yourself as an author brand. Build it by liking other pages and commenting on their posts, posting yourself, and adding news and your own interests. Showing your human side is a good thing but don't show too much opinion or get too controversial.

- ➤ Get to know people on Facebook, **follow** other authors to see how they do it.

- ➤ When your fans find you, be sure to **reply** to them in good time.

- ➤ Post **regular** content – either reposting others' content (picked up from blogs, other social media platforms, news stories, etc.).

- ➤ **Text** posts often get overlooked so try to add an image as well – or create an image specially with the text in it.

- ➤ Get the image **size** right. If images are too small they can't be seen well and if too large they distort and people need to click on them to read them. The current ideal size is 403pixels by 403 pixels – but this can change. Check out the current Facebook image dimensions before uploading images.
  Jon Loomer's website is a great place to get image dimension information (**http://www.jonloomer.com**).

- ➤ If you post a **link** (i.e. a web address/URL), Facebook will generally embed it with an image taken from that site. If it looks good, fine, but if not you can click on it and choose up upload another image. Once the link has embedded it will appear below your post and you can then delete the URL you added earlier – the embedded bit will remain.

- ➤ **Videos** work well on Facebook, they are popular. You can simply post a YouTube URL and it will appear as a little embedded video right on the Facebook newsfeeds of your friends and followers.

- ➤ Don't post too **frequently**, it's not as fast-paced as Twitter (nothing is as fast-paced as Twitter!). Post on Facebook 2-3 times per day maximum, preferably a bit less. You can get away with only posting once or twice a week on your pages.

People tend to unlike pages and people who post too much, they complain it clutters up their newsfeed.

➢ Consider buying some **Facebook Ads**. These can be expensive, unless you use the build-in facility to target your potential customers. Ideally, you want to narrow it down so you have a very small audience – around 20-30,000. That was it won't cost as much because not as many people will be clicking the ad.

Google+

Google+ is something that you are automatically signed up for if you create a new Googlemail (Gmail) account now. Many people find it baffling and don't bother with it but it is worth getting to know.

At the very least, have your basic information on your profile page (like the 'About Me/Us' page of a website) so it can be found if reporters look.

Google+ is very useful for getting indexed by Google. That means you can make a post about each new book you publish – with all the relevant keywords – and it will appear if people search for those terms. Google+ is very important for SEO. If you link to your website on your profile, it will help Google understand that you are a real person/business, not a spammer, and rank your website more highly.

Google Hangouts are also very useful. These are video chats, a little like webinars. You can chat with one person or several, and you can record the whole thing. Post it to Google+ itself, as well as YouTube. Google Hangouts on Air are live and will be broadcast on YouTube and Google+ simultaneously (and recorded). Be sure to tweet about any Hangouts that you do to reach even more people.

HOW TO MAKE THE MOST OF GOOGLE+

➢ Create an account and fill out your *profile*. Add some information about yourself and your books. Upload some photos – a professional one of yourself, your book covers, perhaps some photos that inspire you.

➢ Get to know Google+ by scrolling around and reading others' content. Click *+1* (plus one) on articles you like. You can add a *comment* as well.

➢ If you use *YouTube*, your videos can be automatically posted to your Google+ profile, saving you time but making you look busy on the network.

➢ Use Google+ for *Hangouts*. If you are a non-fiction author you could have a hangout as a training video. If you are a novelist, you could have a hangout where some readers interview you, or you read from your book, or you talk about the inspiration behind your book or your writing in general.

➢ Make *connections* with other users. Your posts will be indexed whether you make connections with others or not, but connections can be good.

There are supportive writer's communities, as well as reading groups, specialist groups, and hobby interests. Show your human side, get chatting about things that interest you.

➢ Join **communities**. They are where much of the action is on Google+. You can find communities that are related to your interests, locality, genres, specific books, favorite authors, or anything you can think of – there are a lot of communities! They are full of people with like interests, so a good place to chat, share content, learn, and build relationships.

➢ People like to learn new things and enjoy getting involved in talking about them. This is where Google+ reigns supreme. Much more than any other platform, you will find lively **debate** on Google+. Keep this in mind when planning what you will post. It may be tempting to stray into controversial subjects because of the debate it can provoke but do bear your reputation in mind. Instead, offer your own knowledge, expertise, [valuable] opinion. Don't get provoked into an argument if someone disagrees with you.

➢ You can use **hashtags** on Google+ and you can also **tag** pages using the '+' symbol followed by the page name.

LinkedIn

LinkedIn is something you should **definitely** be on. It's the social media platform of professionals of all kinds and, as an author, you are – like it or not – a business person. You deserve to have a presence on LinkedIn.

It doesn't have to be grand, just a good professional-looking photograph, your name, website, and some basic information about you. There is a great 'Publications' feature you can add to your profile, where you list your books.

LinkedIn has been around for a long time and has some very powerful people among its membership – so it is very highly thought of by Google and other search engines. If you are a complete unknown, as an author, you can make yourself found very quickly by having a LinkedIn profile and nothing else – not even a website! You can achieve that in a matter of days, just by filling in a quick form on LinkedIn. Your name will come up in a Google search, leading people to your LinkedIn profile, where they can find your contact details, website(s), and information about your books.

LinkedIn is much less informal than all the other social media platforms. Get into 'business' mode before you even visit the site! It is professional, formal, a little straight-laced.

HOW TO MAKE THE MOST OF LINKEDIN

➢ Create an account and fill out your **profile**. You can enter details of your education, workplaces, etc., but don't worry too much about that if your past history isn't impressive! There is a 'Publications' module you can add to your profile with the details of your books – including a sales page link (e.g. Amazon, Kobo, etc.).

➢ Use a professional **headshot** as your photo. LinkedIn has rules about photos. You need to be in business dress, not T-shirt and shorts, and it needs to be a head and shoulders shot of **you** – not your cartoon likeness, your wedding day family group, or your favorite llama.

➢ Make **connections** on LinkedIn by responding to invites and by sending invites. However, there are some rules (like everything on LinkedIn!). LinkedIn don't like spam or dodgy behavior. You can only approach people you are either already linked to via other people or who you know already in some way. You might be asked for the person's email address if you try to send an invite to someone you don't know. When you send an invitation, there is a default message – delete it and write your own personalized one. Only approach people you think will accept your invitation. If the person clicks that they don't know you (IDK = I Don't Know this person), you could be on the receiving end of a snippy email from LinkedIn and – if you get 5 or so - possibly a block on your account.

➢ Don't use the built-in facility to invite everyone in your **email address** book – you could end up inviting the bully from school that you didn't want to ever hear from again, together with your dentist, dog groomer, and an old flame you have been trying to avoid! If you want to build up your contacts really quickly, add *[LION]* at the end of your name on your profile. LION stands for LinkedIn Open Networker, indicating that you won't IDK anyone who sends you an invitation. Don't keep LION on your profile for long, a couple of weeks should be enough to see an increase in your contact numbers.

➢ If you want to use LinkedIn as one of your primary social media networks, you can make **status updates**. These are short messages that you either post on LinkedIn itself or post on Twitter and link your LinkedIn and Twitter accounts. In this way, it is possible to halve your social media time but double your reach as you will have many different contacts on each platform.

➢ LinkedIn isn't the place for **jokes** and Internet banality or photos of cats (however cute they are).

➢ Join some relevant **groups**. These are a covert way of getting to know people without actually being connected to them. You are allowed to approach people who are in the same groups as you.

POWER USER LINKEDIN TIP

Many people have a LinkedIn logo or link on their websites and social media profiles, inviting people to connect. However, anyone clicking the link will have to send you an invitation, they don't automatically connect just by clicking the link. We know that people are much less inclined to follow an instruction if it entails making a number of steps/clicks, so make it much easier for them by creating a one-step invitation link.

1. Go to your profile on LinkedIn. Copy the identification number that is in the address bar (here's mine: **http://www.linkedin.com/profile/view?id= 220089417&trk=nav_responsive_tab_profile** . The 220089417 is the ID number.

2. Paste in your ID number and type in your first and last names into the format of the link below.

http://www.linkedin.com/inviteFromProfile?from =profile&key= 220089417&firstName=Firstname&lastName=Las tname

Here's Michelle's invitation link:

http://www.linkedin.com/inviteFromProfile?from =profile&key= 220089417&firstName=Michelle&lastName=Booth

And here's Nancy's:

**http://www.linkedin.com/inviteFromProfile?from
=profile&key=
164131396&firstName=Nancy&lastName=Hendric
kson**

Feel free to connect with us. If you are asked, Michelle's LinkedIn email is: **michelleboothauthor@gmail.com** and Nancy's is: **nancy@nancyhendrickson.com**.

You can go a step further and use a link shortening service to personalize your invitation link. **http://bit.ly** is good.

Pinterest

Pinterest is a platform that is often overlooked by authors but it is an important one and has a large following. At the very least, **pin** your book covers on there, **follow** some users, **repin** other people's pins, and have a relevant **profile** page.

We live in a very visual society – that's why Pinterest shot up faster than any other social network. Who can't spend hours reading recipe pins, diet tips, watching beautiful landscape photography, or seeing what other pinners are suggesting I read in the mystery genre?

Pinterest is all about images but be sure to add descriptions too. Get the sizes of images right because the bigger your images appear, the better. Images on Pinterest are quite unusual because they are taller than they are wide. If your images are taller they will show up larger on people's feeds. If you post an audiobook cover, they are usually square, so resize it in photo editing software to make it taller.

There is a more technical thing you can do on Pinterest, which needs a developer's help but is worth it. It's called **rich pins**. They allow you to add extra details to things you pin and the *article* pins are of particular interest to us for press releases. We can't profess to understand how to get these working yet – we're talking to developers who are trying to help us get our heads around them!

HOW TO MAKE THE MOST OF PINTEREST

- ➤ Create a **profile** and add your information – be sure to include your keywords, website/blog URL, a little personal information, and about the type of books you write.

- ➤ Set up some **boards**. These are like virtual pinboards. You can name them and add descriptions. Think of things you enjoy, your hobbies, interests, places you like, things you want to do. Add these boards, you will be pinning images to them.

- ➤ Add **pins** – you are 'virtually' pinning images to Pinterest. You can do this by directly uploading them or by pasting in a URL to an online image.

- ➤ **Repin** others' images to your own boards.

- ➤ Fiction and non-fiction writers will approach Pinterest differently. For the fiction writer, we suggest pinning images that are related to your *novel*; pins of the characters, the town, events - make your inner world real but putting a face to it. This technique truly engages readers who want a behind-the-scenes look at how you've so deftly crafted your novel.

➢ Non-fiction writers can create pin boards that help authenticate their *authority* in a specific field. For example, if you write about health, create pin boards on all of the topics about which you write. However, don't forget the personal element; people still want a peek into your real life . . . warts and all!

➢ Use *hashtags* for topics. People search for topics on Pinterest and hashtags are all about topics. Use hashtags on every image you pin.

➢ Be sure to include a *source* when posting images. Fine if they are your own but if you have found them online, included the original URL. Pinterest will often do it for you but it can't if it doesn't know where it has come from.

➢ Include a Call To Action (**CTA**) – e.g. 'Click here for more information' – which will take them to a page on your website.

➢ Always give a *reason* why you are pinning something. That will help get people to engage, repin, and follow your CTA.

> ➤ Add the **Pin It button**[29] to your browser so you can pin easily when surfing the Internet.

> ➤ Use **rich pins** to pin articles if you can get a developer to help you.

YouTube

YouTube has becoming increasingly important and is actually vital now if you want to improve the ranking of your site on Google. Google's ownership of YouTube means that a video is ranked within around an hour of being published.

That means that you new book, which may not come up in an Amazon search for a few days, will come up in a Google search just because you have linked to its Amazon page in a video description on YouTube. This can give a real boost to your book in the important early days. It will also lead viewers to your site and other books.

If you don't think that's important, bear in mind that YouTube is the second most-used search engine in the world (just behind Google itself). It is enormous and very popular.

YouTube even has its own keyword tool – for finding out the top searched terms on YouTube itself. You can find it at:

https://www.youtube.com/keyword_tool

---

[29] http://about.pinterest.com/goodies/

It is very useful to see what is being searched for on YouTube, rather than Google. There are differences. It will give you extra ideas of things to put in your description and tags, in addition to the keywords you use elsewhere.

TYPES OF VIDEOS:

There are a number of different types of videos and methods of creating them. These are some of the most popular:

> ➤ Talking Head – a video of a person talking or demonstrating something. These can be super professional (check out Marie Forleo) or done at home using an inexpensive webcam (a camera attached to a computer) and microphone or iPhone voice recorder.

> ➤ Presentation-based – a presentation done using something like PowerPoint or Keynote can be played while you narrate and record your voice. You can create this as a video very easily using PowerPoint (2010 onwards) by simply saving it as File > Save & Send > Create A Video

> ➤ MovieMaker-based – MovieMaker is free Windows software and very easy to use. You put photographs/images on a timeline and tell them how long to show for. Again, you would record yourself narrating while they play.

> ➤ Animations – hand-drawn animation or doodle videos are popular. Sparkol's 'VideoScribe' is good or you can create your own manually.

IDEAS FOR VIDEO CONTENT

Novelists often have to think harder to come up with content for videos than non-fiction authors. It's possible, though. Here are some ideas for everyone:

- ➢ Press releases – if you don't mind appearing on-camera, record yourself talking about the contents of your latest press release.

- ➢ How To videos – if you write non-fiction you can probably think of lots of ideas for how to videos. Keep them short – 3-5 minutes, ideally.

- ➢ Someone reading a short extract from your book. This could be you, or you could hire someone to do it for you.

- ➢ A cartoon or animal reading from your book. Ideal for children's books. CrazyTalk[30] is ideal software for this.

- ➢ Recorded Google Hangouts.

- ➢ Recorded training sessions or webinars.

- ➢ Uploads of any teleseminars/webinars where you have been the guest speaker.

- ➢ Uploads of any TV or radio interviews that you have done.

- ➢ Podcasts.

- ➢ A 'Meet The Author' recording, where you answer FAQs.

---

[30] http://www.reallusion.com/crazytalk/

HOW TO MAKE THE MOST OF YOUTUBE

- ➢ Create an account and fill out your *profile*.
- ➢ Create a short *trailer* for your book(s) or commission one (there are several good ones on Fiverr[31]).
- ➢ Upload your book trailer to YouTube. Make sure the name of the video itself contains your *keywords* – you can't change the name of the video after you have uploaded it. You can change the title as it appears on YouTube but not the name of the raw file – and it's important to get your keywords in there.
- ➢ Fill out the *description* for your trailer really well. You want lots of keywords in there, but in a natural flow with the text. You can add URLs.
- ➢ Add links to your other videos, if you have any, using *annotations*. You can also add them in the description.
- ➢ Add tags. These are how people will find your video when they search YouTube. Make your first tag your most important keyword. If your books are available in any other languages, get your translator to translate the top keywords into that language and put them as tags too.
- ➢ Choose a good *thumbnail* or upload a special one. Often, thumbnails are too small to see properly and it is better to upload a custom one.

---

[31] http://bit.ly/booktrailerfiverr

It needs a plain but bright background with large, bold text on it.

➤ Take some time to approve, trash, and reply to **comments** that people make on your videos. It's all about building relationships. You can choose whether to allow all comments, hold them for review, or disable comments completely. It's up to you but comments can be quite entertaining and help build your tribe.

➤ **Create** new videos regularly. Keep them short – short videos are more popular. Your videos don't have to be movie quality to be effective. You aren't going for an Oscar, you're going for:

   o SEO – links back to your website.

   o Increased visibility – there are people searching YouTube who don't usually search Amazon but may follow a link in your video description to buy your book.

   o Building relationships.

   o Google indexing.

➤ When you add new videos, **link** to you old ones in them and in the description. Then go back to your old ones and link to the new one. It all helps to get your videos found, which will be promoting your books.

➤ When you have a number of videos uploaded, start using **playlists**. These are collections of things you put together. So have a playlist for each of your book series, your advice videos, your book trailers, etc. When videos are in playlists, when viewers finish watching one of the videos in the list, the next one in the list will play.

TOP TIP:

YouTube experts say you should always make a video *private* or *unlisted* when you are uploading it and adding the description, tags, etc. Go through everything and make sure it's all working well before making the video public.

How Much Time To Spend On Social Media

We would suggest taking the time to establish profiles on all the big social media platforms: Facebook, Twitter, LinkedIn, Google+, Pinterest, and YouTube. Then, choose one to focus on – you can add another later.

Once you have established profiles on the platforms that you aren't going to focus on – which is a matter of just half an hour's work – you don't actually have to post regularly.

Choose the platform to focus on that is most relevant to you, your ideal reader, and your genre.

The table on the next page is a simple guide to show you which platforms could be the most relevant for you.

SOCIAL MEDIA PLATFORM	LinkedIn	Twitter	Facebook	Google+	Pinterest	YouTube
WHAT IT'S LIKE	Highly professional, slightly formal	Fast-paced, short messages	Quite fast-moving but longer messages, with graphics & videos	Attracts Techie people, those keen on SEO. Lots of discussions	Graphical, innovative	Lively, video-based
BOOKS/ GENRES MOST SUITABLE	All, but especially: • Literary fiction • Scientific non-fiction • Medical	All - it's where reporters hang out	All but the most highbrow.	• Technical • Training • How To's • Fiction	• Health • Beauty • Travel • Children • Women's	All - every book should have a YouTube trailer
CONTENT MOST SUITABLE	• Announcements • Press releases • Awards • Milestones • Events • Webinars/speaking engagements	• News • Trends related to your content • Comment • Deals/promotions	• Comment • Events • Author presence • Engagement with fans • Q&As • Book releases	• News • Webinars • Speaking engagements • Events • Press releases	• Cover art • Inspirational photos • [Selected] Personal photos	Almost everything. • Book trailers • Excerpts from novels • Author Q&A • How Tos
POINTS TO CONSIDER	• Keep it formal & professional • Use a good headshot • Has good SEO - link to your website & Amazon page	• You can repeat yourself as content is so fast-moving • Make use of hashtags	• Have personal profile and business pages • Consider using Facebook ads	• Google+ enables you to use Google Hangouts • Have a profile even if you don't post	• Post book covers and link to others • Show hobbies/ interests	• Excellent for SEO • Videos don't have to be professional - can be narrated PowerPoints

Reputation Management

Social media is superb for maintaining your reputation and for handling complaints. It may seem odd to do so in such a public way but it is surprisingly effective. Customers expect brands (and you are an author brand) to respond to complaints and queries on social media very quickly. Some companies employ teams of staff just to monitor their social media streams and respond quickly.

There are some very good examples of things that have gone wrong on social media – as well as things that have been handled very well. We can learn a lot from both!

BRANDS THAT HANDLE SOCIAL MEDIA WELL

DOVE

The beauty brand has had several successful advertising and PR campaigns in the past few years. They handled a lot of it on their various social media platforms.

It has been about boosting women's self-confidence and that's the main reason for its success. Dove weren't seen as trying to promote themselves, they were promoting their customers. Big win all round.

> *Lesson:* Promote others to promote yourself.

IKEA

IKEA have always done well from their product catalogs. Instead of bemoaning the fact that people aren't as keen on printed catalogs now, IKEA simply provided an online catalog via their Facebook page. The result was an increased number of likers of the page and lots of shared posts from people posting about their purchasers. This resulted in new customers and increased sales. Impressive.

> *Lesson:* Don't be a dinosaur, move with the times.

BRANDS THAT HAVEN'T HANDLED SOCIAL MEDIA SPATS WELL

WAITROSE

The U.K. high-end supermarket Waitrose were found to have ordered their egg suppliers to euthanize chickens at just 18 months of age. This caused an uproar with the customers - many of whom were small farmers or people with a bit of land and they offered the chickens homes. Waitrose didn't respond, didn't accept the offer, and refused to engage in discussion.

This just enraged the gentle folk of middle England and they responded by blasting Waitrose's social media accounts with messages and public announcements telling the rest of the public what had happened.

Middle-class shoppers like to think that their pricey eggs are from happy hens, roaming around lush orchards, not hens that are part of a commercial giant's production line, with a short lifespan and uncaring overlords.

They also like to think that their complaints will be heard by the brand that they are loyal to, not ignored and covered up.

> *Lesson:* Don't ignore customer complaints, they won't just go away.

KITCHENAID

KitchenAid posted a dreadful tweet about President Obama's grandmother during one of his debates. They said that Obama's grandmother had known his presidency was going to be bad and chose to die three days before he became president.

KitchenAid immediately deleted the tweet and issued an apology. A senior person admitted that they had allowed a junior to handle the company's social media and that they wouldn't be doing so again!

The problem with social media is that once it has been posted, even if it is deleted, it is still around somewhere. Someone could have taken a screenshot and reposted it. Things like this can go viral very quickly (i.e. widely circulated person-to-person in ever-increasing fashion).

This turned out to be a fantastic example of reputation management in action as KitchenAid managed to turn it around with a few simple actions:

> ➢ Pull the offending material.

> ➢ Apologize – profusely.

> ➢ Have someone senior take responsibility.

> ➢ Learn from it.

> *Lesson*: Only let highly trusted, highly trained people handle your social media.

ODEON CINEMAS

A customer posted a complaint on Odeon Cinemas' Facebook page. He had had a disappointing experience at the cinema, complaining about ticket prices, staff, and noise from a film showing on the adjoining screen.

Not a terrible complaint, it could have been handled with an apology, a couple of free tickets, an explanation, and a determination to do better.

Instead, Odeon didn't notice the post – they weren't monitoring their Facebook page. The post has gathered 25,000 comments and 295,000 likes.

Buried somewhere in those comments there may well be a response from Odeon but what is clear is that they didn't respond quickly enough or sufficiently well. They had a great PR opportunity to put on an amazing cinematic experience for the guy who posted the complaint, to prompt him to post again about his great experience. They didn't. They just left the complaint and all its comment sitting on their page, for all to see and agree with!

> **Lesson:** Act quickly, respond to complaints with tact & professionalism. Use every complaint as a PR *opportunity*.

Authors Who Do Social Media Well

Many authors do an amazing job of managing their social media presence. Space doesn't permit so I've selected just a few who we can learn from.

SHAWN INMON

Shawn is a novelist friend of ours. He has almost 2,000 followers on Facebook due, we are sure, to his regular humorous comments. Here are few:

When one door closes and another one opens, you might call those Ghost Hunter guys. Your house may be haunted!

Am I the only adult that still tries to use The Force to pick up my silverware?

While Dawn is gone overnight, I might do silly things like see if that chemistry set I got in 1970 still works. Pretty sure I can get that all cleaned up and the ceiling repaired before she gets home.

He's a naturally funny guy. You may not be, no matter, you will have some personality strength that you can draw on. Don't be afraid to post the odd personal comment but get your family's permission first if you're tempted to mention them!

Perhaps you are devoted to animal rescue charities or you are a keen musician. Draw on those things to show your true personality and you will draw like-minded followers who will become – like Shawn's – your loyal tribe.

CHERYL KAYE TARDIF

Cheryl is a Canadian thriller writer who wrote *How I Made Over $42,000 in 1 Month Selling My Kindle eBooks*. In the book, she tells the story of how she used Twitter to help market her books:

> *"How do you use Twitter to market your eBooks? Simple. You create relationships ... By showing a genuine interest in people, you'll gather more followers. Eventually, some will read your book. Maybe they'll tweet about how much they enjoyed it. Maybe they'll suggest it to their book club, or to a producer they know. This actually happens."*
>
> Cheryl Kaye Tardif

Cheryl's strategy is, like Shawn's, to use her personality strength. She is genuinely interested in people. She's sociable and friendly and that comes across in her social media posts.

MIGNON FOGARTY

Mignon is the author of *Grammar Girl*. She says she enjoys spending time on social media and suggests that other authors:

> *Find the social media platform that you enjoy and do that – even if it isn't the most popular. Don't be afraid to ask people to buy your books. If you have spent hours of your time answering readers' questions you have earned the right to market your products.*
>
> Mignon Fogarty, quoted on
> The Write Life blog[32]

At the other extreme, she says she sees a lot of authors jump into Twitter and immediately start doing nothing but push their book. They haven't earned the right to market their products, and all they do is turn people off.

---

[32] http://thewritelife.com/how-successful-authors-use-social-media-to-sell-more-books

The lesson we can learn from Mignon is to spend more time building relationships than marketing your books.

Handling Trolls

There are haters out there – when they are online they are known as trolls. They seem to come out of the woodwork more readily on the Internet than anywhere else, thinking that it gives them anonymity. However, the courts take a dim view of threats, whether verbal or written and things written on social media are there forever. They are searchable and retrievable by law enforcement agencies.

Some celebrities have closed social media accounts because of what are popularly known as 'trolls' – people who post nasty comments online.

If this happens there are a couple of things you can do:

> ➢ Act quickly.
> ➢ Block the person from posting on your page/profile and/or sending you messages.
> ➢ If they have been threatening, take a screenshot of the message and store it. The police will be interested.
> ➢ Don't ever respond in kind. Keep professional, keep polite. Don't engage in any kind of insult-throwing, especially on a public page.
> ➢ If you are going to threaten legal action, do it privately – in a private message (known as a 'direct message' or 'DM' on Twitter).
> ➢ If the unpleasantness was on a public page, post

an apology to everybody who had the misfortune of reading it and say relevant action has been taken. It's a good time to thank the rest of your community for their support.

➢ Remember that there are far more good people than trolls.

The Golden Rule Of Social Media

Never, ever post on any of your social media accounts when you aren't in a good state of mind. That could be depression, having had a few drinks, or when you've had bad news.

Authors need to maintain a certain mystique, while being seen to be honest and open. It's a delicate balance.

PR isn't just about sending out press releases and posting on social media. It's about protecting your reputation by avoiding things that could spoil all your efforts.

It's fine to be real but don't get too real. Remember that you are a brand and you need to protect your reputation.

For that reason, never comment on reviews or reviewers on social media either. It won't make them look bad, but it will make you look terrible.

CHAPTER SEVEN

THE PR POSSIBILITIES OF BOOK CATALOGING SITES

❧

OOK CATALOGING SITES ARE POTENTIAL online goldmines for authors. They are large databases that list books. Readers join them to catalog their own books and discover new ones to read. So they are full of *readers*, people who love books. The very people we want to connect with – but we have to go about it the right way, or we risk alienating them.

Firstly, we simply need to have a presence on the three main book cataloging sites. Then we need to make sure our books are them. That makes our books more available for readers to discover. Just as it isn't enough to have Amazon's large database list our books, though, it isn't enough to put our books on cataloging sites and leave them. We need to take steps to make them more visible.

We can't do that in an overt way though. The best and only way to be successful at PR on the book cataloging sites is to be on them as a reader, first and foremost. Members of these sites are very put off authors who just join to push their own books, who don't join in, don't stick to the rules (official and unofficial), and who only show up when they have a book to promote.

The three main book cataloging sites are:

> Goodreads
> Shelfari
> LibraryThing

Of these, only LibraryThing is independent, the others are owned by Amazon.

At the very least, establish your author profile on each of the sites and 'claim' your books so that you are listed as the author.

We need to be seen as readers on the book cataloging sites, chatting, getting involved, meeting people. That doesn't mean we need to spend hours and hours on them, we just need to log in occasionally to:

> Like and comment on other people's posts.
> Add new books to our shelves.
> Note where we are up to with the book we have said we are currently reading.
> Enter some competitions.

> Add a blog post.

It isn't rocket science and it doesn't take long.

If you decide to focus on one site, Goodreads is probably your best bet, unless your readership is very Indie and anti-Amazon, then LibraryThing would be for you.

There are some very simple things to remember when using these sites and they are common to all three:

> Don't go in with the "Buy my book" message.

> Talk about what you *read* much, much more than what you write.

> Don't comment on reviews/ratings – ever. It's the mark of an amateur author and is looked down on by readers, publishers, and other authors.

> Don't recommend your own books to others, even if the site lets you. Instead, do it subtly by using things like Listopia on Goodreads and the free eBook facility on LibraryThing.

> Don't send a blanket message to any book bloggers you come across on the sites. They are good places to find book bloggers but you need to do it professionally. Check out each blog and be familiar with what they write about before contacting them.

There's a very interesting article[33] on 'InsatiableBooksluts' blog (it isn't a vulgar blog but they have picked a curious name!) about the way some authors use Goodreads. They mostly complain about authors commenting on their own reviews – and getting into unfortunate public arguments.

The comments on the article are very revealing. One complains about the number of authors who send 'Half price sale' announcements to everyone who has entered a competition (known as a 'Giveaway' on Goodreads) to win their book.

The commenter herself says that she won't read any author who doesn't have a full [virtual] shelf of books, proving themselves to be as avid a reader as the rest of the community. She points out that an author who doesn't read much is unlikely to be an author who writes well.

So the big things to do on book cataloging sites are:

Add Lots Of Books To Your Virtual Shelves

Have a selection of books that you have read, are reading, or intend to read listed on your virtual shelves of the book cataloging sites. These should be from a wide variety of authors and genres, including your own.

---

[33] http://insatiablebooksluts.com/2012/05/11/the-authors-guide-to-social-media-goodreads-how-to-tell-if-youre-doing-it-wrong/

It's a good idea to have your competitors' books on your shelves. Aligning yourself with them is a good strategy.

Don't Comment On Reviews Or Ratings

Don't even read them, if you think they might enrage you. It just isn't worth the damage to your reputation. PR is all about your reputation – why spend building it up only to damage it with one unfortunate comment to a troll reviewer? Rise above them.

Be Seen

Just adding a book to your shelf, clicking like on someone's blog post, or voting on a book in a Listopia puts your profile picture in front of your connections in their newsfeeds.

Being seen around book cataloging sites shows that you are an author who reads and that you are approachable. Readers love that.

Take Advantage Of The Unique Features Of Each Site

On Goodreads you can use Listopias and Giveaways, on LibraryThing you can offer a free eBook, on Shelfari you can add extras to your books. A Goodreads giveaway, in particular, is a wonderful thing for getting your book found. These things get your name and your books seen around the site and that bring very valuable benefits.

Keep an eye on the sites for any new developments, as they are all keen to keep their share of the market and come up with new things regularly.

You don't need to spend hours on book cataloging sites, just pick your favorite and check in once or twice a week.

CHAPTER EIGHT

THE PR POSSIBILITIES OF YOUR WEBSITE

ᘓ᙮ᘔ

I F YOU DON'T HAVE A WEBSITE ALREADY YOU might want to think about starting one. It's an inexpensive but supremely valuable platform for you as an author.

The easiest and quickest way to build a website yourself is to use WordPress. WordPress started as a blogging platform but sites created using WordPress can look like regular websites. They have the dual advantages of being very popular with Google and being easy to update yourself, without needing to hire a designer every time you want to add details about your latest books.

Even if you aren't technically-minded, you can have your own WordPress-powered site. Hire someone on

Fiverr or PeoplePerHour to set up your site for you. All you will need to do is buy the domain name – your site's address or URL – and some hosting (we both like Bluehost and HostGator for hosting). Then give the details of those to the person who is going to install WordPress for you. You can change the logins afterwards to keep it secure.

Nancy wrote a popular book about WordPress[34] which walks you through the process of installing it yourself if you would like full control. It really isn't difficult, so many things are one-click now!

Your website is like your store window. It allows people to search for and find you, quickly and easily. It provides yet more social proof that you are who you say you are. A reporter receiving your press release will often Google your name. If they do, they should find multiple mentions of you in the search results, including at least:

- ➤ Your website.
- ➤ Your LinkedIn profile.
- ➤ Your Amazon author profile.
- ➤ Your Goodreads profile (more on that later, under book cataloging sites).
- ➤ Your individual books' Amazon and other sales pages.
- ➤ Your press releases, listed on various sites.

---

[34] http://amzn.com/B00AEB5EHE

How To Make A WordPress Site Look Less Like A Blog

The only problem with a WordPress site is that – out of the box – it looks very much like a WordPress site! Blogs are great but they don't look like slick, professional websites, without some tweaking.

You might want to keep your site looking like a blog, and that's fine, but be sure to choose a pretty theme to make it look good, and to post frequently.

If you want to make it look less blog-like, the first thing you can do is to have your home page – the page that people see when they first visit – as a static page, not as a page showing your latest blog posts.

Do this by creating a welcome page then going to Settings > Reading and choosing your new welcome page as the Static Page instead of Latest Posts.

You can also remove the WordPress link in the footer by going to Appearance > Editor and opening Footer.php. Remove the line that refers to WordPress. You are altering the theme here – don't panic if anything goes wrong, you can just reinstall the theme to fix it!

Experiment with different themes because some look more like regular websites than others. Don't chance using free themes (except from people you trust) as they can be buggy and can be a way in for hackers. The same goes for plugins, only get them from reputable, highly-recommended sources. A subscription to a

WordPress theme provider is a good investment. ElegantThemes[35] is a good one.

Be careful with your widgets. Often WordPress themes automatically add a widget block so you can sign into your site easily. This really isn't necessary as you can just add */wp-login.php* to your site's URL to get to the admin login page.

Dealing With Spam

Anyone who has a website will have to deal with some level of spam. This could involve spam emails, because you have your email address published on your site (use a sacrificial email account so the spam won't get mixed up with your important emails).

Often, it will involve spam comments on a blog. These can be a real nuisance. The reason for most of them is because the spammers want a link back to their site from yours. We've already looked at how important it is having other sites pointing to yours, in terms of how the search engines view you. So spammers make comments on blogs all over the world, trying to get links back to their own dodgy sites!

One way to deal with spam comments in WordPress is to use an anti-spam plugin. We like the 'Stop Spammer Registration' plugin. It is free and easy to use. You can search for it from the Plugins section of your WordPress site.

---

[35] http://www.forauthors.info/themes

Some high profile bloggers are turning comments off completely, rather than face the hassle of dealing with spam. Michael Hyatt is one[36]. He makes the point that social media conversations have become more widespread and important than blog conversations (comments). It's a fair point. if you don't want to deal with comments you don't have to, just turn them off in the Discussion panel of your WordPress dashboard.

Add Your Press Releases

When you produce a press release you will probably distribute it via one or more online press release distribution services. You will no doubt also post about it on social media. Those posts will have to go to the distribution service URL though – unless you also upload your press release on your website. Then you can send people back to your website to read your press release and hopefully they will also read other things on your site, sign up for your newsletter, notice your Goodreads reading widget, etc.

Here's how to do that.

> ➢ Format your press release beautifully and convert it into PDF format.

> ➢ Upload it to your website (very easy if you use WordPress).

> ➢ Create a 'Press Room' page on your site.

---

[36] http://michaelhyatt.com/pulling-comments.html

➢ Type in the name of your press release on the Press page and hyperlink to your PDF press release.

➢ Keep creating press releases, uploading them, and linking to them on your Press page.

Link To Your 'Information Central' From Everywhere

Use your website as 'Information Central' about you and your books. Again, we're thinking about social proof here. Google will notice that you are also mentioned on Amazon, Facebook, and Twitter as the author of X book, so it must really be you, and not someone masquerading as you. It will also note that other sites are linking to yours (Twitter, Google+, LinkedIn), so your site must have some importance. It will therefore make your site appear higher in the search results when people search for your keywords.

So fill out your profiles on all the big social media platforms and on the 3 main book cataloging sites: Goodreads, Shelfari, and LibraryThing. All those links coming back to your site are super important.

Keywords Rule

Always be thinking about keywords. Keep lists of them – for yourself (premier llama hairstyle author) and for your books (llama hairstyles, llama grooming, camelid care). Sprinkle the keywords throughout the pages and posts on your site, as well as in the titles and captions you add to any photos, videos, or audio you upload. Also use them in tags, if you use WordPress.

The titles of the posts and pages on your website are very important. Pages are the more solid, forever things, the structure of your site – they are the things that appear in the site's menu: e.g. Home, Books, Press, Resources, Speaking, etc. The posts appear on the framework provided by the pages. They are the ever-changing things that you will add over time. Both posts and pages are indexed by Google and other search engines, and posts in particular have the potential to go viral. One way to help that is to choose really good titles for them.

One expert on keyword-packed titles is author, actor, and creativity coach Bryan Cohen. In a 'Conversations About Marketing[37]' interview with book marketing expert D'vorah Lansky, Bryan stressed the importance of strong post titles. He suggested writing titles that people care about, and that have keywords in them which people will search for. He said:

> *One post that got a lot of traffic was 'Five Essential Tips for Lazy Writers'. I knew that that kind of a title would get people interested because it's kind of funny.*
>
> Bryan Cohen

---

[37] http://conversationsaboutmarketing.com/guest-expert-series-bryan-cohen-30-blogs-in-30-days-virtual-book-tour/

Bryan also recommends having a 'Speaking Engagements' page on your site. Here you can list any talks you have done already. These could be a chat in a reading group, a talk at a library, a workshop at a school or hobby group. Keep adding to your Speaking page. Note the dates of your speaking engagements as they are very easy to forget later on! Include photos if possible and link to any relevant external sites. These could be the library or school's website.

Having a website has always been a good idea for authors but it is becoming vital. Not having one is ignoring a valuable piece of real estate.

The website 'The Writing Platform' has a great article[38] by Simon Appleby where he evaluates 10 author websites. It's worth going through the article to read his thoughts about the good and bad points of each site. You could also look at the websites yourself to see if you can pick up any ideas for your own. He makes an excellent point:

> *Hopefully there's not a writer alive who doesn't believe they need a website – there are so many good reasons for having one that even if you don't agree with all of them, you ought to agree with one or two.*
>
> Simon Appleby

---

[38] http://www.thewritingplatform.com/2013/02/ten-author-websites-that-really-do-the-business/

What Else Should Be On Your Site

➢ A **lead magnet**. That's something you give away free (a virtual something - for example a short eBook, report, audio recording, or video) in return for visitors' email addresses. You can stay in touch with your visitors and build up a relationship with them. Link to your lead magnet in your books too, it's a way of staying in touch with readers. People who have bought something from you are likely to buy again, so you can let them know when you release future books. Use a service such as MailChimp[39], Aweber[40], or GetResponse[41] to create an attractive form that links to their email software. The form goes on your site as a widget.

➢ Either a page containing a list of your **books**, or a page for each book. Be sure to include links to all the places you book is available for sale – not just Amazon.

➢ A good **bio**. Include some photos – a professional headshot, such as the one you use on LinkedIn, as well as some less formal ones, perhaps of you with your children or dogs. Shots in nature go down well. A friend of Michelle's who is a well-respected social media expert in the U.K. used to use a photo of herself peeking around a tree. When she changed it to a more 'respectable' one

---

[39] http://www.forauthors.info/chimp
[40] http://www.forauthors.info/aweber
[41] http://www.forauthors.info/getresponse

she was deluged with complaints! Don't be afraid to share some personal information such as your writing day, your interests, your favorite charities. Just don't share too much location-specific information – such as names of clubs you attend.

➢ **Press page** – your press releases, of course, but also links to any mentions your books have had on blogs or other sites. Interviews that have been published with you (or that you have sent!) in newspapers/magazines. Publications you have appeared in.

➢ **Speaking Engagements** page – a list of your speaking engagements, with dates and links.

➢ **Contact Me** – either an email address (invites spammers) or a contact form (JotForm is good), together with social media links.

➢ Your **Blog** – or a page listing all your blog posts.

➢ **FAQ** – add questions and answers here that people may want to know about you, or have already asked. This is gold for reporters and readers alike.

CHAPTER NINE

WHERE TO FIND PR MATERIAL

ভ৪৪১

IT'S EASY ENOUGH TO FIND PR MATERIAL FOR your book launch press release but what's next? There are lots of things you can do to find things to write about, both in press releases and on social media. Just remember to make 80% of your social media posts about others and only 20% about yourself/your books.

The content of your press release could be sparked by something you see in a news alert. Write it from your perspective as an expert author in that genre, making your comment on it. Then repurpose it for social media.

It is fine to create a press release containing your comment on a news story – it happens all the time. Don't be daunted by the term 'press release', it's just a way of getting potential content out there for reporters, bloggers, and other social media users.

This chapter is about finding content to post on social media, which shows that people are actively looking for content. If you send it to them in the form of a press release, or post about your release, you are providing valuable content to other social media users – free!

Here are a few ideas:

Google Alerts

We've mentioned Google Alerts already but it's worth repeating because they are of such value. Sign up for them at:

http://www.google.com/alerts

Create alerts for as many things as you can think of in relation to you and your books:

- ➤ Your name.
- ➤ Your pen names.
- ➤ Your book titles.
- ➤ Your main keywords for yourself and your books.
- ➤ Your interests.
- ➤ Your book themes.
- ➤ Your town.
- ➤ Your region.

You can choose to get alerts as it happens, once a day, or once a week. Set these according to your schedule. We're both full-time writers so having them come in once a day works well for us. Any more than that could get irritating and any less could mean we miss something newsworthy. News isn't news the day after the event.

When you get the alert emails, go through them to see if there is anything you could comment on in the form of a press release, or just do a link to the original source from a social media post.

There are alternatives to Google – Mention[42] is one. It has a free option and several paid levels, starting at $9.99 per month.

Blogs

Follow blogs that relate to the genres you write in. They will probably have good articles of their own, as well as guest posts, news, and competitions. These are great fodder for social media posts.

Approach good blogs to see if they would be willing to have you as a guest blogger, or would publish an 'interview' with you (that you supply). This can be great for getting more traffic and links to your own website and you can post about it on social media.

---

[42] http://www.mention.com

Newspapers/Magazines

It's a good idea to read a popular newspaper regularly – either online or in print. Something like the Huffington Post has a huge readership, which shows that its content is popular. Find stories in it that you can link to on social media, or respond to in the form of a press release.

Find newspapers and magazines in the genres you write in, as well as in your interests and other areas of expertise. You can also comment on news stories. Michelle commented on a news story in a popular British newspaper one day and saw her book sales spike! She hadn't mentioned the name of her book, just 'a book about xyz'. It's a powerful technique – don't over-use it. Keep everything you write positive and informative. An article[43] on the InsatiableBookSluts blog could help you keep yourself in check!

Slideshare

Slideshare[44] is a LinkedIn-owned site that began with the goal of sharing knowledge online. It certainly does that, it is one of the top 120 most-visited websites in the world.

People upload presentations – made in something like PowerPoint or Keynote or, increasingly, using the free app HaikuDeck. Often, these are professional

---

[43] http://insatiablebooksluts.com/category/series-2/authors-guide-to-social-media/
[44] http://www.slideshare.net/

presentations from thought leaders and experts. There is terrific content on there and it is all free.

Scroll through to find things relevant for you and your readers, then post a link to the relevant presentation, add a comment, interview yourself in video format about it, etc.

Social Media

You can find lots of stories on social media itself that you can re-purpose. This is easy on most of the platforms by retweeting (Twitter), sharing (Facebook), pinning (Pinterest), etc.

Some of the groups/communities are useful sources of content too. Infographics are good to share, as are graphs/charts of all kinds.

Quora

Quora[45] has, like Slideshare, the aim of sharing knowledge. Whereas Slideshare uses presentations, Quora uses questions and answers.

It's a place for you if you are an expert on something – anything! – but it is also a good place to find content. You will find tons of questions that can spark ideas. You can also post questions yourself, as a type of informal market research.

---

[45] http://www.quora.com

Tom Corson-Knowles has published an inexpensive Kindle book[46] about how to use Quora for marketing purposes.

Your Website

If you have had your website for a while, you may have a surprising amount of content on there that you can re-use. If you have an author website for any length of time, at some point you will be approach by book publicists or authors to ask if you would be willing to let them do a guest blog or interview. This is great material for very little work! If you have done some, you can post about that, turn it into a video, add it to Pinterest with the author's photo, and more.

You may have other interesting things on your site. Have a look through and if there is anything that you can re-purpose.

Repurposing Content

You can share the same content on different platforms if you mix it up a bit – change a text post to an image post, an image post to a video, etc.

Also, post content at different times – remember that people are in different time zones. This is particularly applicable to Twitter, where people don't mind duplicate content. You might post a link to your latest press release at 7am on Twitter. You can post it again a hour or so later on Twitter, that's fine, but you can mix

---

46 http://amzn.com/B00BZIREY6

it up by using a different hashtag on the second posting.

You can then post the same link on Facebook around noon, but with a relevant image as well.

If you have written blog posts before, or have several articles stored up that you haven't' put out yet, you can:

- ➢ Write a blog post.

- ➢ Find a suitable royal-free image and upload it with your blog post.

- ➢ Get the URL of the blog post and pin that on Pinterest, which will show the image.

- ➢ Record yourself talking about the subject, or reading your blog post. Post this on social media platforms.

- ➢ Make a PowerPoint or Keynote presentation about the topic – you only need a few slides – and record yourself talking while you play it. Format this as a video and upload it to YouTube.

- ➢ Upload the presentation to Slideshare and share that on LinkedIn, as well as on social media platforms.

CHAPTER TEN

EXAMPLES OF GOOD PRESS RELEASES

 C3 80

HERE ARE THE LINKS TO SOME BOOK RELEASE press releases on PRLog that have generated a lot of views – so they are getting something right! We'll look at a few of them in depth but it is worth you checking them all out to see if you can use any of the ideas in terms of keyword location and the 'hook' in your own releases.

http://www.prlog.org/12289325-willie-stewart-releases-novel-tarnished-to-critical-acclaim-using-groundbreaking-unconventional-promotions.html

http://www.prlog.org/12287490-poet-leonard-roller-debuts-darklight-poetry-collection-book-combining-cosmology-astronomy-humor.html

http://www.prlog.org/12242607-spoiled-expat-and-blogger-releases-new-novel-the-amsterdam-confessions-of-shallow-man.html

http://www.prlog.org/12148714-colorado-author-releases-thrilling-adventure-novel-inspired-by-mountain-living-in-gilpin-county-co.html Definitely keyword-inspired - adding the inspiration for the novel, mountain living – people will be searching for mountain living).

http://www.prlog.org/12237822-contemporary-womens-fiction-novel-discusses-choices-one-woman-has-to-make.html

This is a great one. It isn't saying 'new novel by', it is talking about the content – excellent format to follow.

SUMMARY

WHETHER YOU LIKE IT OR NOT, IF YOU ARE an author you are a business person – a brand. If you are an introvert, it kind of helps to think of yourself as a brand.

Rather than feeling you are talking about yourself – which can feel odd – you are talking about your brand. Your brand is what you need to promote to feed your family, keep a roof over your head, and have a secure future. It takes the pressure off to think of it that way. You should find yourself more about to come up with ideas for promoting your brand – more than if you were thinking about ideas to promote yourself!

If you are an extrovert, you have an advantage because it will be easier for you to get yourself 'out there' on videos, guest spots, podcasts, etc.

If you do appear on-camera/screen, it is worth chatting to a style/color expert to find the best colors for yourself and – both sexes – the best makeup. Cameras can wash us out and we've all heard the old adage that the camera adds 10lbs. Getting some advice beforehand can give you the confidence you need to shine, knowing that you're looking your best.

Michelle was buying some new makeup and, in chatting to the sales lady, mentioned that she was getting it prior to having some professional photos taken. The lady told her she was buying the wrong makeup! She explained that there are different finishes and you don't want a very matt makeup if you are having photos taken.

So if you're going to be on-screen, a visit to a department store with a big beauty department might be a worthwhile trip. The consultants are trained in all types of makeup application and can give guys and gals great advice to help them look their best. You can also telephone the counters and ask for a makeup consultation – which is often free. They can do your makeup for a video and you don't have to buy anything – but be warned, you will probably want to!

If you're going to New York Times bestseller status, a consultation with a professional stylist is a must. ColorMeBeautiful[47] consultants are able to give advice on color, shape, hair, eyewear, jewelry, makeup, and more. They aren't the only stylists, of course, but they

---

[47] http://www.colormebeautiful.com

are the only ones we have had experience of and so feel confident recommending.

Your Regular PR Activity

You need to be aware of your brand's reputation, protect it, and do everything possible to improve/maintain it. You are also your own PR and media spokesperson, and your own marketing department – coming up with the marketing plan for each book and being aware of and responsive to news and publicity opportunities.

You can do this by the use of:

- ➤ Regular press releases for:
  - o Book launches.
  - o News comments.
  - o Book updates.
  - o Announcements – speaking engagements, video releases, guest spots on webinars, etc.
  - o How To's.
- ➤ Regular use of social media for:
  - o Daily (or at least a couple of times a week) posting, engagement, and interaction on your favorite 1 or 2 social media sites.
  - o Keeping your profiles up-to-date as you release new books, embark on joint ventures (perhaps a book with a co-author or participation in an authors' event), do speaking engagements or blog tours.

- o Responding quickly to any news stories that are relevant to you, your books, and your best keywords.
- ➢ Regular use of book cataloging sites to:
  - o Add your books.
  - o Interact with others.
  - o Be seen as a reader – add others' books to your shelves, review them, talk about them.
  - o Use their tools to promote your books.
- ➢ Monitoring online mentions of yourself and your books by:
  - o Setting up Google Alerts or other online monitoring services for your name, any brand name(s), your book names, any series names, and your best keywords.

Evaluation Of PR

One thing that we haven't gone into too much (because it would require another whole book) is evaluation of PR, to find out if it is giving adequate return on investment (ROI).

In an agency situation, an account handler could be responsible for presenting information to their client to show how their PR campaign was working. This would involve keeping a file of press cuttings (often an online collection or document), details of engagement on social media (hard to evaluate in just numbers but this often involves numbers of followers, likes, etc.), and details of reviews, customer feedback, and more.

This is less important for us as authors because we aren't dealing with huge sums of money here. We don't have to leap into action if we notice that an expensive campaign isn't having the desired effect.

We do need to keep an eye on what is working for us and what isn't, though. Even though PR activity is often free, it does cost time and time is valuable.

It's important to keep an eye on which of your PR activities are working well and which aren't. Switch things around occasionally and test to see what changes.

Perhaps you chose Goodreads as your book cataloging site to focus on but realize after a few months that most of your sales are coming from Smashwords rather than Amazon. If that's the case, you would be better going with LibraryThing, as your readership could be anti-Amazon.

Maybe you decided to focus on Twitter rather than Facebook as your favored social media platform. You might decide to switch to Facebook so you can get to know it in order to use Facebook ads – which can be very effective.

It's good practice to keep records of your book sales, which many of us do with pleasure – it's great to see those figures rising! If you keep a spreadsheet of sales, it's easy enough to add another couple of columns to document your PR activity.

So if your sales were $500 in March and you distributed 3 press releases but only $200 in April and you didn't distribute any press releases, you might want to write a few more releases!

APPENDIX 1

PR CHECKLIST

CR80

When You Launch A Book

BEFORE THE LAUNCH:

Keyword research – make a list of the most-searched keywords that relate to your book's title, content, and inspiration.	
Write your **launch press release** – find the hook or story.	
Send your launch **press release** with **ARCs** (advance review copies – digital or print) to relevant reporters, bloggers, and reviewers.	
Do several **blog posts** about your writing	

process and inspiration behind the book.	
Do social **media posts** about the book, mentioning the publication date, story behind it, tips from it, etc.	
Order or create your **book trailer** and post to YouTube.	
Post the YouTube book trailer link on your **social media** accounts.	
Update your **LinkedIn** profile with the information about your latest book, together with purchase links.	
Assemble lists of **reporters** and other media contacts – use Twitter, LinkedIn, Google searches.	

AT AROUND THE TIME OF THE LAUNCH:

Send a book launch **press release** via a distribution service.	
Send the launch press release to named **reporters** and other media contacts from your own or bought-in lists. Find reporters who write in the same niche as your book.	
Get the URL of the press release (from the distribution service) and post it on **social media**. Post it several times a day for a few days on Twitter, once everywhere else.	

Get friends, other authors, and people you have done favors for to **post** about your book!	
Update your Goodreads, Shelfari, & LibraryThing profile with the details of your latest book.	

AFTER THE LAUNCH:

Monitor **Google Alerts** for mentions of your book. Respond to (thank) bloggers and other authors who mention your book.	
Monitor the **news** and other sources such as blogs for mentions of things that are relevant to your book's content or your expertise. Respond by:	
Continue writing occasional **press releases** about **news** topics that are related to your book's content/story.	
Posting about news topics on your website/blog, social media profiles, etc.	
Monitor online **newspaper** sites, especially ones that allow comments on articles, for things that are relevant to your book or expertise. Comment where appropriate – as an expert in the industry. Someone may look you up on Amazon.	
Post **reviews** on Amazon and other book	

sales sites on various books but especially within your own genre(s). Have your Amazon reviewer name as '... author of XYZ'. ALWAYS be positive, even if you need to be [mildly] critical.	
If you are comfortable on-camera, post some *video reviews* of other people's books. They are fairly unusual so attract attention.	
Upload regular *SlideShare* presentations – as a way of raising your own/your book profile and of adding subscribers to your email list.	

APPENDIX 2

MARKETING PLAN

CR&D

YOUR PR PLAN SHOULD BE PART OF YOUR overall marketing plan. Give this careful thought and research, learning from observing other authors, publishers, publicists, etc.

Your marketing plan could include:

> **Keyword research** – we can't stress enough how important it is to know your best keywords. These are the words/phrases that people will use to find your book.

> Your own **website/blog** – install analytics on it so you can see where you visitors are coming from, your most popular pages, how long people stay. In this way, you will be able to improve your site and will know in which areas you are most popular. You can then advertise in those

areas if you wish.

➤ **Building a list** – write a short eBook to give away free on your website in return for visitors' email addresses. The list of email addresses is valuable. You can email people, send newsletters, ask for beta readers/reviewers, etc. Don't neglect your list, work on building it. Use a service such as MailChimp (free) or Aweber (paid) to maintain it for you.

➤ **Creating your 'brand'.** Not just you as an author but also a brand for each of your book series or the genres you write in. Get outside help if you can afford it – even if it's just Fiverr gigs.

➤ **LinkedIn** profile, posts, and community (group) activities.

➤ Other **social media** platforms – profiles, posts, pages, lists, and ongoing activities.

➤ **SlideShare** presentations. There is a new [free] tool that helps in making cool presentations suitable for SlideShare. It is called HaikuDeck[48] and it takes the pain out of trying to find suitable images for slides. The most popular SlideShares – and, increasingly, the ones that get featured on the front page – are those with strong, full-slide images. You can find them easily in HaikuDeck. SlideShare is a great way of getting sign-ups to your email list. Have a simple call-to-action on the last slide in your presentation, offering

---

[48] https://www.haikudeck.com

something free when people sign up.

➤ **Book trailer** – doesn't have to be amazingly professional, just get a trailer and fill out the description for great SEO results.

➤ Add your latest book to your Amazon **Author Central** and other book sales profiles.

➤ Fill out the book's **sales page on Amazon** and other book sales sites (if you aren't enrolling in KDP Select). Use your keyword research to sprinkle the relevant keywords throughout the description. Format it using HTML on any sites that let you (Amazon does).

➤ **Book covers** in various formats – Kindle, print, audio.

➤ Set up a **blog tour** or find another author to host on your own blog.

➤ Plan your initial week's **price** – we suggest $0.99 for the first week.

➤ Join and post in **author groups** on Facebook that allow posts about free or bargain books.

➤ Schedule a **promotional offer period** – free or a Countdown Deal (KDP Select), or a reduced price.

➤ Alert **sites** about your free or bargain days (use Author Marketing Club's free book submission tool[49], which lists the latest sites that allow free days submission).

---

[49] http://authormarketingclub.com/members/submit-your-book/

➤ Send out **ARCs**[50] to reviewers and book bloggers.

➤ Send **emails** to reviewers, book bloggers, other authors, asking if they would post an interview with you (send a press pack containing a press release, professional photograph of yourself, and FAQs). Don't be afraid of this, many bloggers are glad of content that they can post – it saves them work!

➤ Update your **book catalog sites** profiles – claim your latest book (e.g. Goodreads, Shelfari, LibraryThing and other specialist book cataloging sites).

➤ Add **book extras** about your book on Shelfari. Novelists are fortunate here – you can add extra background information about your characters, inspiration, deleted chapters, etc.

➤ Schedule a **Goodreads Giveaway** for your print book. Support it with some [paid] Goodreads ads around the middle of the period.

➤ Post the first couple of your chapters as a **preview PDF** on Goodreads.

➤ If you aren't in KDP Select: Offer your book on **StoryCartel**, in order to get extra reviews.

➤ Have a **virtual book launch party** on Facebook – invite other authors (and reciprocate when they invite you to theirs).

➤ Add some information about your book to your

---

[50] Advanced Review Copies – these can be print or digital

email signature. Include a link to its sales page or pre-launch press release.

➢ Consider some **paid advertising** on Facebook or book sites such as **BookBub**.

➢ Approach local **bookstores** to ask if they will consider stocking your book.

➢ Plan and create some **YouTube** videos based on your book or Q&As with you. Be sure to fill out the descriptions with as much text as they will let you, including keywords and URLs to your other videos, website, etc.

➢ Make good use of social media and **repurpose** content all the time – turn old blog posts into new videos, turn videos into podcasts, create new posts from news stories and use a few quotes from these to make images to post on other platforms.

➢ Look up **DaysOfTheYear.com** to find unusual events and celebrations that may relate to your book. If there are some, plan a press release a week or two before and send to some newspapers. You will need to send the release several months before for magazines – they have much longer schedules for their contents.

APPENDIX 3

PR DO'S & DON'TS

❧

A GOOD FRIEND[51] WHO IS A PR GENIUS WAS kind enough to spend hours and hours bringing Michelle up-to-date with the do's and don'ts of PR in the modern era. When she had left PR before going into teaching, the Internet hadn't been invented – she had a lot to learn!

PR is so much better now. Practically, press releases used to have to be put in envelopes manually, addressed, and mailed - now it's one click of a button! Morally, people are more about helping each other for mutual benefit rather than stepping on others to get to the top.

There are disadvantages, too. Reporters and editors, like the rest of us, get hundreds of emails every day so

---

[51] Amanda Jackson from Tigerfish PR: ttp://tigerfishpr.co.uk

it is very easy for yours – containing your precious press release – to get lost in the crowd.

It's also quite common to pay for placement now – something that was hardly ever done back in the 80s.

Michelle's friend gave her some top tips, some of which we have included here, together with others that we have both picked up along the way. Let's start with the negative ones – because they are the most important and the ones that can trip you up if you're not aware of them:

Don't

> Use your **name** in the headline. You can include your **book's title** but don't make the headline just the book title.

> Use industry **jargon**.

> Use **exclamation marks**. It doesn't make you look humorous, it makes you look illiterate!

> Include **book reviews** in your release. You can refer to one by using a few words as a quote but no more than that.

> Send a press release or photograph as an email **attachment** to a busy reporter – unless they are expecting it. If you're spoken to them and they've requested a photo or more information, then it's fine to send an attachment but otherwise don't do it. They are busy, busy people and don't have time to download and open attachments (which can be in various odd

formats, requiring them to open different software programs).

➢ Request that a reporter sends you his/her copy for **approval** before publishing it. Just isn't happening!

➢ Ever say "**No comment**" when asked a question by a reporter. It makes it look like you have something to hide. It's better to say that you don't have anything to add yet but will update them as soon as you know anything. It makes you look open and honest rather than furtive and worried!

➢ **Delay** if a reporter rings you. They are working to the clock, they have very tight deadlines. If you can't give them a story/clarify something, they'll move onto someone who can with alarming speed. If you get a voicemail, ring back straightaway.

➢ Assume anything you say is **confidential**. If you are going to say something that you don't want them to write/broadcast don't say it. They could forget which bits of your conversation were supposed to be confidential, or they could just be desperate for a good story and use it anyway. Sometimes a reporter in all good faith omits certain things from his/her copy but the editor finds them and adds them. Be safe, keep quiet about delicate things.

➢ Tell a reporter/editor that anything you say is **off the record**. This is similar to not assuming confidentiality. They're busy people, they just want the information they can report, not what they can't.

➢ Try to tell a reporter **what to put** in his/her story. They will decide on the most important points to highlight.

➢ **Telephone** to ask if a reporter/editor has received your press release. It just ticks them off. Most reporters will tell you it's their pet hate. Many of them receive hundreds of press releases every week. If everyone rang to follow up their release, the average reporter would spend all their time fielding calls and have no time to write.

➢ Try to **pitch** to reporters via **social media**. It feels manipulative and most of them don't like it. A press release is more upfront. They are generally on social media anyway so do use it but direct approaches are tricky. Social media is about being social, making relationships. Start up a conversation instead, not a direct sales-type pitch.

Do

➢ Remember that your press release is about a **story** that a reporter might want to run with. It isn't about you or your book but the story behind the book. Avoid self-promotion.

➢ When you refer to yourself, use your **full name** the first time, then your **last name** only on any further mentions. E.g. 'New book by Stephen King' initially, then 'King says ...'.

➢ Always refer to yourself in the ***third person*** – don't say "I".

➢ Check your ***formatting***, ***spelling***, and ***grammar*** several times before distributing your press release. Ideally, get someone else to read over it for you.

➢ Check your ***facts*** and make sure any ***URLs*** you have included lead to the right place.

➢ When sending your press release by email, use your press release's ***headline*** as the ***email subject line*** and the body of the press release as the body of the email (never as an attachment0.

➢ Offer to send ***photographs*** if the reporter wants some. They like this, it saves them money by not having to send a photographer. If you are speaking to TV reporters, call them 'visuals'.

➢ Be aware that a reporter may want to ***ring*** you to do a telephone interview if you have sent them a press release. Add all your contact numbers to the release/email so they stand a chance of getting hold of you.

➢ If a reporter telephones you for an interview or further information, stick to the ***facts***. Don't speculate or repeat industry/social media rumors.

➢ On the same theme, keep your ***answers short*** and to the point when talking to reporters. They are short on time, they don't want to hear your long-winded opinions on everything from the weather to the economy.

➢ Have a ***backup person*** who reporters can contact if you aren't available. This could be a media savvy friend or fellow author, an eloquent relative who has worked in a marketing department, a PR agency that you pay by the hour.

➢ Show that you ***know their work*** (if you do – if not Google it). Compliment them on their reporting of something they did recently and you'll have them eating out of your hand!

➢ Maintain good channels of ***communication*** so you can be verified by researchers and reporters. In particular, have a good website, a presence on LinkedIn, and regularly post on one or two social media platforms.

FURTHER READING/ VIEWING

ognoso

Susan Cain's TED talk, which Bill Gates named as one of his favorite of all time:

> *http://www.ted.com/talks/*
> *susan_cain_the_power_of_introverts.html*

15 LinkedIn Profile Picture Blunders

> *http://www.socialmediacoach.ca/blog/*
> *93-15-linkedin-profile-picture-blunders.html*

Cautionary Tales For Authors From A Book Blogger:

> *http://insatiablebooksluts.com/category/series-2/*
> *authors-guide-to-social-media*

Help A Reporter Out - Become an expert on **HARO** and receive daily alerts of the stories that reporters are looking for people with your expertise. From $19pm.

> *http://www.helpareporter.com/sources*

SourceBottle

This is like HARO but in Australia. It costs $25 per month for the pro level but there is a free level. You receive 'call outs' when reporters want someone to interview with your expertise.

http:// www.sourcebottle.com.au

Press Release Tips From Mynewsdesk

http://insight.mynewsdesk.com/en/tips/
news-journalists-will-read

Days of the Year

http://www.daysoftheyear.com

Copyblogger article – 8 Ways A Digital Media Platform Is More Influential Than Marketing

http://www.copyblogger.com/digital-media-
platform

Mr Media Training – Brad Phillips has tons of useful articles and videos on his site for media training of all types.

http://www.mrmediatraining.com/tag/brad-phillips

WHAT NEXT?

 C3℘

I F YOU ARE EITHER EXCITED ABOUT STARTING A big PR campaign for your books or terrified and wondering where to start, we have a few things that may help.

When To Get Professional PR Help

When Michelle ran a training center, she wasn't surprised to discover that one of the most successful centers in the national network was paying around $3,000pm to a PR agency. It raised their profile and enabled them to hit national and regional news regularly. It was one of the factors that made them so successful.

They had to reach a level of success first, of course, in order to be able to afford professional PR help. Until they did, they had handled their own PR.

If you have the determination, you should be well able to manage your own PR until you're ready to hand over the reins to a professional. So when should you think of hiring an PR agency or professional book publicist?

Ultimately, it's your call and depends on your budget and level of comfort in handing over the handling of your publicity campaigns. The following milestones could be a guide that it's time:

➢ You have 6 or more successful books in one genre/series, each selling 10 copies per day or more.

➢ One of your books has hit the big time in terms of national publicity and awareness.

➢ You are getting spots on national radio or TV.

➢ You are receiving daily requests for interviews, guest blogs, podcast spots.

Book publicists and PR agencies that specialize in supporting authors can be expensive but they are worth the money if you have a number of existing successful books and are likely to produce more. A top-class PR campaign can turn you from a successful author into a celebrity author.

Do get advice from other authors before signing up to an agency. You will need to know exactly how they have supported authors in the past to gauge what they can do for you.

Agencies have staff who specialize in 'presenting' to potential clients. They are flash and professional. They will treat you like a VIP and baffle you with inflated assurances, proof of the success of previous campaigns, and their 'excitement' at the potential of handling your important account. It's vital not to allow yourself to be impressed with their glossy promises. Remember that they are trained to impress and sell their agency over others.

You need:

> ➤ Hard facts, not meaningless brochures.

> ➤ A feeling that you could get along well with your potential account manager. Don't contemplate an agency that doesn't introduce you to the person who would be handling your account. Ideally, you want one named person in control and several others also working on your account. Remember that agency staff could be working on many different accounts. You want to feel that they value yours highly enough to keep a close eye on it and on potential news opportunities.

> ➤ Solid proof of the success of campaigns for authors similar to you.

> ➤ A flexible contract that you can get out of quickly and easily if things don't work out.

> ➢ A flexible payment system. Perhaps you will only want their support once or twice a year, not every month.

We can't stress highly enough the importance of networking with other authors in situations like this. Getting a recommendation about an agency first-hand from an author you trust, who you know is very successful, is vital.

Facebook and LinkedIn groups are wonderful for making connections with other authors.

Use A VA

If your books are doing well but you're not yet in the position to hire a PR agency, you might consider taking on a Virtual Assistant (VA).

One of the most successful authors who we know personally who uses a VA is Steve Scott. Steve is very busy and decided to try taking on a VA to help with the more routine tasks of his business[52], including research and publicity.

You can find a VA on any of the people-hiring sites such as PeoplePerHour, ODesk, and Fiverr. Or you could advertise on CraigsList or another site/publication in your country.

---

[52] We firmly believe that Steve is so successful because he thinks of himself as a business person rather than 'just' an author. He knows that if he doesn't promote his books, they won't sell. He isn't just an author, he's a marketer and that gives him a $4,000+pm income.

A VA can free you up to write more, which is ultimately your best way of earning more, long-term.

One of the biggest tips we can give for working with a VA is to invest some time in writing detailed instruction manuals for all your main tasks. You may not think you have any but you probably do. For example, every time you publish a book, you probably add it to your Amazon Author Central account, your Goodreads and/or Shelfari accounts, and add the details of it to several other sites such as BookGoodies. You may choose to enroll in KDP Select and schedule some free promo days or Countdown deals. You will need to publicize these by submitting the details/dates to as many book blogs/sites as you can find.

These are all things a good VA can do – and do well.

Next time you publish a book, try writing down your main tasks and see which you could write up with detailed instructions in order to hand over to a VA.

CRAD

That's the end of the book. We hope you have enjoyed it but, more importantly, we really hope you will implement some (or all!) of the strategies we have suggested.

You can get going right now by setting up Google Alerts to start monitoring the Internet for potential stories to respond to and/or write press releases about. Start compiling lists of reporters (especially by milking the

Twitter lists of big PR agencies!). Get plenty of releases out and keep writing them.

Join in events, network as much as your natural introversion/extroversion will let you – online or offline or both. Make the most of social media. Support other authors in their PR efforts – many will return the favor.

Persistence pays. Keep at it.

Most important of all: think of yourself as a business person. That's what you are – like it or not!

Thank you so much for reading our book. If you have enjoyed it, we would be delighted if you could spare the time to write a few words of review on Amazon and/or add it to your shelves on Goodreads.

BOOK BONUS: EXCERPT FROM GOODREADS FOR AUTHORS

CHAPTER 1 GOODREADS OVERVIEW

 GOODREADS CALLS ITSELF: "The largest site for readers and book recommendations in the world." It certainly is large, with 440,000,000+ books listed. It is a huge site – you will keep finding new things even after using it for a few years!

Their membership doubled in the year from 2011 to 2012, from 6.5 million users in 2011 to 13 million in 2012. It reached 25 million users in 2014 and continues to grow.

It is larger than Shelfari (another Amazon-owned book cataloguing site) and LibraryThing (an independent book cataloguing site) combined.

The idea is for users to list the books they are reading, have read, and want to read, so that they can recommend them to others.

It is more than just a book recommendation site though. It is possible to form book clubs (with people from all over the world, which is pretty cool - imagine discussing 'Wild Swans' with people in China!), write & read reviews of books and compare books with others. There are now over 20 million reviews on Goodreads.

The site was founded in 2007 by Otis Y Chandler, a software engineer, and Elizabeth Khuri Chandler, a journalist and editor. They are very active on the site and it is possible to friend both of them.

Otis – the great-great-great-grandson of the founder of the Los Angeles Times - had noticed that he loved looking at his friends' bookshelves to see what they had read (I'm with him on that!). He thought it would be a great idea to create a site with virtual bookshelves so people could not only see their friends' bookshelves but also find out what they thought about all the books they had read.

The result is a very comprehensive, easy-to-navigate site that is rapidly growing in popularity – both among readers and authors.

How It Is Similar To Facebook

If you are familiar with Facebook you should be able to get used to Goodreads very quickly.

Facebook profile = Goodreads user profile

Facebook page = Goodreads author profile

Facebook friends = Goodreads friends

Facebook page fans = Goodreads author fans

If you aren't familiar with Facebook it doesn't matter – you can get started on Goodreads quickly and easily without a huge learning curve, just by following the instructions in this book. Goodreads says that Facebook and Twitter aren't the most popular places for people to find new books, and the statistics support that.

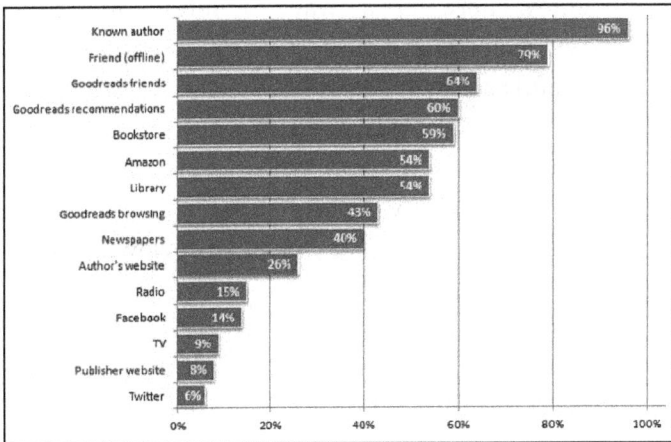

Source	Percentage
Known author	96%
Friend (offline)	79%
Goodreads friends	64%
Goodreads recommendations	60%
Bookstore	59%
Amazon	54%
Library	54%
Goodreads browsing	43%
Newspapers	40%
Author's website	26%
Radio	15%
Facebook	14%
TV	9%
Publisher website	8%
Twitter	6%

Where people discover new books
Source: The Goodreads Blog

Only 6% of people claim to have discovered new books on Twitter and just 14% on Facebook.

How It Differs From Amazon

Authors know that reviews sell books. Goodreads is full of reviews but you can also write reviews on Amazon, so why would you choose Goodreads?

There are some very compelling reasons:

> It is easier to follow reviewers on Goodreads. There are no alerts on Amazon. If you read a fantastic review of a book, then read and love the book yourself, you are more likely to want to follow that reviewer's other reviews on Goodreads. It makes sense – you don't waste money on books you aren't going to enjoy. There is a way to follow Amazon reviewers but it isn't obvious. It is also less useful as not all Amazon reviewers stick to one genre or style. You are more likely to find good Goodreads reviewers who specialize in the type of reading you like.

> Goodreads will notify you when reviewers you like post new reviews.

> Goodreads works as a social network – Amazon is purely a sales site. Goodreads is a sort of Facebook for literary-minded people. You get to make relationships, discuss books, discover others. Amazon is more of an impersonal shop window.

> ➢ On Goodreads, you can display the books you have read on a virtual shelf and allow others to explore them.

For authors, having a presence on Goodreads is an excellent idea. You are able to find out what people are currently reading and enjoying, what's popular, which authors have good followings, how the bestselling authors are interacting with their readers, and much more.

Once you start making friends on Goodreads, you can make relationships, build trust, and write reviews. You will naturally gain a following and those people are much more likely to buy your own books – then review them.

As in business, people buy from people. We are all more likely to read a book if a trusted/similarly-minded friend recommends it. *So getting on Goodreads and making friends is the most important first step.*

There are other, more powerful reasons that you should consider being on Goodreads, though – as well as spending both time and money on the site:

> ➢ CBS News reported that part of the explanation for the popularity of '50 Shades of Grey' was because of Goodreads.
> ➢ Publishers take notice of Goodreads. Berkley bought 'Bared to You' (a '50 Shades of Grey'-type novel) and cited its 2,500 reviews on Goodreads as a major reason.

➢ Users visit the site frequently (one statistic says more than twice per day) and spend 4.4 minutes per visit.

➢ Every day, there are 10,000 reviews written, 2,800 book recommendations, 22,000 giveaway entries and 2,300 authors 'fanned' (these statistics[1] are from 2011, so will have grown since as the site has expanded rapidly). Every time someone does something with a book – shelves it, rates it, reviews it, comments on it – it shows up in their friends' [Goodreads] feeds and possibly on their social media profiles.

➢ The average active Goodreads user has shelved 54 books, written 10 reviews, has 35 friends, and has 19 books on their To Read shelf.

➢ The community includes readers, booksellers, librarians, book bloggers, teachers, and authors..

➢ 21% of all Goodreads users have a BOOK BLOG. Is your author antenna standing to attention? Mine was when I read that the first time.

---

[1] www.slideshare.net/PatrickBR/using-goodreads-to-promote-your-books

OVERVIEW
IF YOU'RE IN A HURRY

- ➢ Goodreads is social – not sales. Social sells because it is relationship-based and people find it more trustworthy.
- ➢ You can browse the bookshelves of other authors, potential buyers and existing readers.
- ➢ Establishing an author profile on Goodreads gives you more access to potential readers.
- ➢ Goodreads can propel your book into viral-type popularity.
- ➢ You can do valuable, informal market research by seeing what the current and forthcoming trends are, using discussions, polls and other features.

If you would like to learn more about how to use Goodreads, you can find Goodreads for Authors on Amazon, in Kindle, print, and audio versions.

ABOUT THE AUTHORS

Michelle Campbell-Scott

Like many authors, Michelle has been through a number of careers (advertising, public relations, teaching, training). She prefers the idea that this has brought a wealth of experience to her writing rather than the fact that she is a bit fickle.

She wrote training courses and articles for other people for many years before plucking up the courage to enter the publishing arena under her own name(s). She learned the necessary skills from Cathy Presland's 'Publish Your Book On Kindle' course (*http://bit.ly/kindlecourse*) and published the first book under her own name in 2012.

Her books include:

- 7 Myths About Aquaponics (as Michelle Booth)
- Goodreads for Authors
- PR for Authors
- Make Your Book Work Harder (with Nancy Hendrickson)
- Mo: The Talking Dog (as Michelle Booth)
- The 10-Day Skin Brushing Detox (as Mia Campbell)
- Inversion Therapy (as Mia Campbell)
- How Henry VIII Got Fat (as Mia Campbell)

She also has courses on Udemy:

- Electronic Shorthand (*http://www.forauthors.info/eShorthand*)
- Goodreads for Authors : Book promotion & marketing (*http://www.forauthors.info/prgr*)
- Learn how to get your book on CreateSpace (*http://www.forauthors.info/prcs*)
- Email Marketing for Authors (*http://www.forauthors.info/csemail*)
- Learn how to create a beautifully-formatted eBook *(http://www.forauthors.info/cssigil)*

Michelle is from the north-western UK and is currently on a roadtrip around the US and Canada.

Nancy Hendrickson

When she was a child, Nancy wanted to be an archaeologist, but instead fell in love with the power of words.

She was traditionally published until she discovered the financial benefits of self-publishing.

Her books include:

- How to use Evernote for Writing and Research
- Writer's Block: Vanquished Using Images, Oracles and Brain-Hacks
- How to Write for Kindle
- 35 Must-Have iPhone & iPad Apps for Awesome Pictures
- WordPress Websites: Beginner's Guide to Easily Building a Website & Customizing It With Themes and Plugins
- Finding Your Roots Online
- Beginners Guide to the Sun
- Pinterest – Build Your Brand, Your Tribe, Your Sales
- Freelance Success: Write Your Way To A Dream Lifestyle

Nancy lives in Herb Cottage in San Diego, California.

INDEX

Y